Praise for *The Heart's Alphabet*

James Grimm has not only written a captivating life story, he's managed to create a new kind of autobiography—a sort of chamber music in which he acts as conductor as family and friends, admirers and grateful caregivers, all add their brief riffs to his own powerful account of his remarkable life. Jim Grimm is a witty, sly fox of a writer, unpredictable and delightful as well as inspiring. He's that rare being—a genuinely charismatic person. What a surprising joy to meet him in this riveting memoir that opens a door to a hidden life rich in love and adventure and life's most affirming emotion—gratitude.

PATRICIA HAMPL
I Could Tell You Stories: Sojourns in the Land of Memory

To call James Grimm's book *The Heart's Alphabet* a unique work is an understatement. Born with cerebral palsy and unable to communicate verbally, Jim tells his story and the story of those significant others who have been part of his life. *The Heart's Alphabet* is a story of courage and persistence, about a man who chose to defy the odds.

JOHN SCHWARZLOSE
President and CEO, Betty Ford Center

The Heart's Alphabet isn't just the story of a person living with disabilities. It's rich on insight into the human condition and told with eloquence, honesty, wit and wonderful humor. Jim Grimm can't live without the supports provided by others, yet it's clear he has given his family, caregivers, friends—and all of us—even greater gifts. What an amazing man! What an amazing story! Enjoy each challenge, adventure, insight, and wondrous turn of phrase.

BRUCE NELSON
Executive Director, Association of Rehabilitation
Resources in Minnesota (ARRM)

On the Government Activities and Advocacy Committee for United Cerebral Palsy of Minnesota, James' insight into public policy positions helped to promote the full citizenship of people with disabilities. *The Heart's Alphabet* tells a frank and honest story that people with cerebral palsy and every parent of a child with a disability should read. This book will show them that they are not alone in their desire for independence. His fears, frustrations, depression, desires, joys and triumphs remind the reader that people with cerebral palsy should be treated with respect and dignity. His memoir provides us with a glimpse of what it means to "be trapped in a body you cannot control" and yet have the same hopes, dreams, and desires as every other person on earth. James is very fortunate to have a very supportive family and close circle of friends and caregivers who have provided him with opportunities some of us can only dream about. Jim is an inspiration to all! Thank you for sharing your story and life with us.

Jo Ann Erbes
Executive Director, United Cerebral Palsy of Minnesota

The Heart's Alphabet contains a most profound message, a universal truth for all of us. We are so much more than the physical body we inhabit on this journey called life. Jim makes clear that we are all called to look into each other's eyes and see the soul and choose to love. I heartily endorse Jim's book! Let yourself laugh and cry a little, but most importantly learn a lot! You will see that we are all so much alike.

Beverlee Hood R.N.
Palliative Care, Hospice

The Heart's Alphabet

DARING TO LIVE WITH CEREBRAL PALSY

James Grimm

TASORA BOOKS

ISBN 978-0-9789946-7-9

Cover design & photo section layout: David Spohn
Book design: Wendy Holdman
Printed in the United States of America on acid-free paper,
at BookMobile, Minneapolis, Minnesota

To order additional copies of this book please go to
www.itascabooks.com

To my parents Gordy and Esther, my brother John, and sister Mary for helping me live such a good life

To my caregivers and friends for trying to help me live a normal life

For everyone who has put up with me while trying to complete this book

To Lucia Hamilton and Damian McElrath who have been so patient with me while assisting with this book in all its aspects—both the writing and editing. I also want to thank Richard Solly for editing and David Spohn for layout and illustration.

Finally I am grateful to all have contributed with thoughts of their own.

Contents

Prologue

I AM JIM GRIMM. I have cerebral palsy, a birth defect caused by damage or faulty development of the motor part of the brain that disrupts the ability of the brain to control muscular body movement and posture. I am forty years old, have quadriparesis, have been unable to speak verbally my entire life, yet I have communicated eagerly to all who would listen. I have much to say, and this book is my story.

Foreword

WHAT DO YOU SAY, and how do you say it? That's my challenge in sharing thoughts about James. Working as a therapist with James over the past twelve to fourteen years has been very meaningful. Therapists learn from their most challenging or unique clients. My relationship with James is different from those I have had with other clients. Being able to come to his home and see him where he lives provides a deeper level of understanding than would be possible in a clinical setting. Seeing him with his caregivers, advocating for his needs, or exposing his vulnerabilities gave me an appreciation for how individuals with chronic illness or disabilities live. Every day. Each week. Month after month. Personal cares and daily functioning.

We first met in Cambridge, Minnesota when James and his father came to our first session. Dressed in a Chicago Bulls shirt, James was a young adult man "trapped within his body," preventing him from openly communicating with the world in conversation and advocating for his needs. He was clearly very bright, and his mental status was sharp as a tack. He had a great range of interests and a very loving, close relationship with his family. In a way I saw James as a person who was stuck behind a one way mirror, observing everything, hearing everything but unable to verbalize and share his thoughts and opinions spontaneously. I've often said that James could produce a home video series titled "The Tricks of Stupid Caregivers and Helping Professionals" for the enjoyment of all of us! Interpreting for Jim through his limited communication style has allowed for meaningful discussion and the exploration of dilemmas and problem solving situations. As we developed our therapeutic relationship, I gained a tremendous appreciation and respect for the challenges James has endured and continues to face.

Think of the challenges! How do you communicate in a world of conversation and computerization without the use of your voice or hands? How do you emphasize things that are important without intonation or spontaneous verbal exchange? How do you trust caregivers in the intimate closeness of meals, personal hygiene, and personal cares when they may be new to your staff or you are having difficulty with how they are doing their jobs? How do you manage coping with your body as it refuses to do voluntarily as you would wish? How do you demonstrate patience while relying on others to do for you those things that others can do for themselves? How do you experience your own sexuality as a single adult male interested in women and desiring the closeness of an intimate relationship? How does James manage? How would you or I manage?

James has asked me to write a Foreword to his book. *The Heart's Alphabet* is a most appropriate title. Through our journey together, James has shared with me many stories and intimate feelings and opinions about life, love, family, and day-to-day concerns. He is an honest man, a sensitive and caring man.

For those who read this or know James and his family,

there are many stories to share. There are stories of how close and caring the Grimms are as a family. There are stories of concerts, games, or special events that James has gone to. There are stories of caregivers who are close and committed to providing the best care on a daily basis for James. Stories of how important are the team of professionals who have worked and advocated for James and his family. Stories of James' friends and the importance these friendships play in his life. There are many stories to tell. For me, James is truly a special person, facing challenges I cannot even imagine. He is blessed with great parents and siblings who have advocated for him and supported his desire for as much independence and self-determination as possible. James has grappled long with the question "Why Me?" and found meaning and purpose in living with his disability. He is at peace with issues of his own immortality, while seeking to grab and enjoy all that life has to offer. His story is one of possibilities for people born with a life-long disability. A story of incredible perseverance, joy, and meaningful relationships with others. A story of a life of meaning, passion, and purpose.

Paul Sherman, M.S., L.M.F.T.

PART ONE

Speaking My Mind

ONE

The Early Years

EVERY CHILD IS SPECIAL. My parents, Esther and Gordon Grimm, had certainly learned the flexibility necessary to raising children with unique gifts and personalities as happened with their three children of whom I was the third. However, I was destined to be the one who most challenged their parenting skills.

My entry into the world on February 1, 1967 was dramatic. I had a quick breach birth, was bruised from the waist down, and was on oxygen for the first twenty-four hours. I was jaundiced and had difficulty nursing. My parents knew immediately that something went terribly wrong. I had lost all muscle coordination. My body was rigid; my muscles constricted in continuous spasms. I had no control over my reflexes and could not assume a sitting position. I did not want to sit in an infant seat and did not develop motor skills the way most children do. My parents sought advice from numerous doctors, but received little support initially. My mother is a registered nurse, yet her concerns were brushed aside. She was called a "nervous mother." Another doctor told my father, "He'll never play football, but he'll be fine." My parents struggled with inconsistent medical advice and were often very frustrated and sometimes angry in the process.

The reality is that in the mid to late sixties, the medical profession did not know much about cerebral palsy. At age two, I was finally diagnosed as either having cerebral palsy or being mentally retarded.

Although I couldn't talk, I was a bright, alert child. I understood everything people were saying, and my disability did not prevent me from communicating. By age three, I smiled for positive things and frowned at negative ones. Later, I learned to use my tongue, the one muscle that I could command, to communicate.

They say "no man is an island," but a child with a disability needs a larger community than most. I was born in Chisago Lakes Hospital and grew up in Center City, Minnesota, a small town about forty-five minutes from the Twin Cities of Minneapolis and St. Paul. My mother, as I mentioned, was a registered nurse. My father is a retired Lutheran pastor and was the director of training and health promotion for the Hazelden Foundation, a world-renowned center for chemical dependency treatment. If God picks special parents to raise a child with cerebral palsy, I was certainly advantaged. My parents were loving, patient, and tenacious in their drive to give me every opportunity to live a normal life.

However, many other people supported their dream and gave generously of their time. During a one year period, four volunteers came to my house four times a day to help "pattern" my muscles by taking me through exercises designed to train other parts of my brain to supplement the mid brain area that was destroyed. A total of sixty people were involved with my therapy. Although this experimental technique called the Domain DeLacatto Method proved ultimately fruitless, it helped keep my muscles limber and gave me much social contact. When I went to nursery school at the Curative Workshop, many of these same people volunteered to chauffer me. They would drive me down to Minneapolis where I would have one-and-a-half hours of physical therapy and a half-hour of occupational therapy. Then I would spend time on typical nursery school activities such as painting and puppet shows. Later, they would drive me back home. I was the most severely physically disabled child in my group. However, the support of my family and community encouraged me to be independent. I attended pre-school at Michael Dowling, a school for children with special needs, with the help of volunteers who drove me. Today children are fortunate to have many services that weren't available back then.

A key highlight of my childhood was our family's trip to England in 1972 when I was six. We were there for a year on a sabbatical my father had taken to study at the University of Birmingham. We lived at a Lutheran Retreat Center named Hothorpe Hall in a Manor House. This is where we met the Sundheims. While there, we had the opportunity to visit Germany, Norway, Scotland, Belgium, Switzerland, Sweden and Wales. The tours of castles, cathedrals, and other historic sites made lasting impressions. I met wonderful people in Europe. I would encourage others to live abroad to experience life from a new perspective. From my experience, I gained an appreciation for how fortunate we are to live in the United States with all its advantages. I was a small child and in a stroller at that time of my life. However, my parents had to carry me in many places that were not accessible. When we visited a castle in Cotswold, Devonshire, my dad carried me up 130 stairs! I am sympathetic to those who live with physical disabilities in places that are not well adapted to their needs. It makes life so much more challenging.

While riding in a car one day in England with my older

brother John and my sister Mary, they told me to stick out my tongue. I did. This "game" quickly progressed to a more challenging level, as siblings often do with each other for amusement and to pass the time. They commanded me to stick out my tongue 100 times, and I did, exactly 100 times. Now we had learned something! I knew how to count and I had one strong muscle, my tongue, I could command at will. It was a breakthrough.

My tongue connected me to the world. My family and I devised a communication system to help teach me how to spell. They would say the alphabet, staring with the letter A, and when they had reached the appropriate letter, I would stick out my tongue part way meaning "yes." This method of communication continued to help me spell out first words and then sentences. This worked similarly when they wanted to ask me questions. My tongue part-way out meant "yes," and stuck out all the way meant "no." With our eyes locked together, we would slowly but effectively bring out my thoughts into speech. To this day, this process continues and has been my connection to the speaking world for over four decades.

TWO

The School Years

WHEN WE RETURNED from England, I started first grade in a regular school. I was one of the first mainstreamed students with a disability in Minnesota. I am proud that as a child confined to a wheelchair, I overcame significant physical challenges to attend a regular school. Although there was an elevator in the school, there were no other handicapped-accessible curbs, bathrooms, or drinking fountains. I did have an aide, however, who worked with me one-on-one. I encountered well-meaning teachers, some who were enlightened and some naive. This is where I met Jim Kelly who was my speech therapist and now one of my best friends. The thing a child with a disability wants most fervently in the world is *not* to be seen as different. Instead, he wants to fit in. Some teachers realized this and some didn't. One of the more uncomfortable experiences was a fourth-grade teacher instructing my classmates to say "hello" to me each morning. I wanted to squirm, but couldn't. If I could have, I would have crawled under a desk, but I was trapped. Another teacher who stands out though in a positive way was Mr. Ness. He treated me awesomely! I was just a normal child to him, and I am so thankful to this day for his consideration. Mrs. Sellman, my sixth-grade teacher, also was remarkable in her approach. It is a gift when a teacher can treat a child as unique but normal. These teachers and others saw that I was normal in every way except my body. They saw past my disability, respected my thoughts and feelings, and encouraged my talents.

My ability in math, as evidenced by my tongue-counting talent, blossomed early. When I was nine, my mother and I would sit curled together on the floor; and we would multiply three-digit numbers together. Math was a game that came easy to me. I later learned to apply this skill and a steel-trap mind in a more productive way to my passion for sports. I became well-known even in grade school for my knowledge of sports statistics. In fact, teachers used me as a resource before betting on games. To this day, I challenge anyone to beat my command of sports trivia.

I love sports, and although my body prohibited me from running bases or throwing a ball, I still participated. In eighth grade, I asked to be the assistant manager of our football team. I devised a number of plays, and one in fact that was very helpful to the team. Difficulties shouldn't stop someone from enjoying life and doing the things they love. I celebrated our wins with the rest of the team and commiserated on our losses just as like any other sports-crazy boy.

Throughout my life, my family and I have held out hope that technology would help me communicate and live more independently. We tried numerous methods. When I was eight, I got an electronic communication system that was operated by my left leg. However, it was too hard to control my leg as well as my head and spell all at the same time. Later on, my family learned about the Trace Center at the University of Wisconsin where I was evaluated and given a foot switch. This too proved unworkable. When I was in seventh grade, we tried a more sophisticated and creative form of communication. I went to the new Communication Center at the Courage Center in Minnesota where Ray Fulford, an engineer at the center and his team, devised a tongue switch for me which proved to be too difficult. I learned to use the switch with Morse Code to spell out letters. A specially devised computer program allowed my messages to print on an Apple computer. It was a great idea, and I was initially very excited about the possibilities to communicate my thoughts independently. I was determined to make this work.

I then went to Gillette Children's Hospital where Marty Carlson, the head of rehabilitation, and his staff worked tirelessly to design switches to make me both ambulatory and able to communicate with the world. I had to learn over 1,000 combinations of three-digit numbers, which stood for letters and words. These were transmitted via a tongue switch or toe switches to a computerized voice synthesizer. However, after several years and three or four different tongue switches, I eventually lost interest in it because of the difficulty I had in maintaining my body position and head control and in using the tongue switch all at the same time. It was a big disappointment.

For the last twenty years, I have been working with Marty Stone, an engineer, on a computer that has a head set that clicks on a letter when I move my mouth. This is still in development due to funding issues. I also tried using an electric wheelchair with a switch on the left side, near my leg. I had fun with the knee switches because at last I could go off by myself in my electric wheel chair, but I would either get stuck in the mud, go in circles, or bump into shelves at the stores. Unfortunately, here too there were problems despite lots of effort. Muscle spasms in my leg made it too difficult to be a practical solution for me. Still, I am so thankful for the many, many people—engineers, technicians, family members, friends and caregivers—who have tried tenaciously and applied much creativity over the years to help me live an independent life.

I was confirmed in 1983 at Chisago Lakes Lutheran Church. Laney Brottem was a great friend who helped me study and do my confirmation lessons. Junior High was a lot of fun. I had many friends, including my first girlfriend, Jenny. We knew each other since first grade. Jenny and I went to a lot of dances together. We are still in touch today. Another friend from Junior High was Traci Lambrecht. Traci is now a beautiful woman and writer who uses the name P.J. Tracy as a pseudonym. In fact, the crime scene investigator in her books *Monkeewrench* and *Live Bait* is named Jimmy Grimm after me.

In the classroom I got good grades and consistently made the honor roll. In ninth grade I was in competition for the highest grade point average with another student. I am proud to say that I received the award. School work was challenging due to the difficulties imposed by my disability, but with the help of others, not impossible. My aides would take notes for me and read my assignments aloud to me. Although I can read, it is hard for me to keep my head in one position for very long; and I am unable to turn pages. My tests were done orally with my aide reciting the alphabet until I could compose my answers. It was a slow process, and required determination (something I have a lot of). Some teachers were not aware that I was smart. They made assumptions about my mental ability based on the fact I couldn't talk. It was very frustrating for me to encounter that prejudice. Fortunately, a guidance counselor knew how smart I really was, and we had a good understanding with each other. This support encouraged me when I was down, and I got good grades, consistently making the honor role.

I graduated with a "B" average and an academic letter, presented to me by the football team. When I went up to receive my diploma at graduation, the audience gave me a standing ovation. It made me feel great because I worked so hard to get my diploma. My Dad was asked to speak at my graduation. He thanked the school and the whole community for their support. There was not a dry eye in the auditorium that afternoon.

My mind sometimes got me into mischief, too. My class had a reputation for being the "baddest," and I certainly contributed to that. One time my friend Don and I put glue on a teacher's chair. However, I was usually not a suspect and never went to detention. That was one case where being handicapped had its advantages! Sometimes, the teachers also got involved in small pranks. One time, a teacher hid me from my aide, Teresa. All in all, I liked high school, especially world history.

During those years, an important event was a trip to San Diego as a guest of Joan Kroc, the widow of the late Ray Kroc, founder of McDonalds. Joan knew my family through the Hazelden Foundation, where she had donated money for a sports training and education center. My parents had Joan over for dinner one night when I first met her. I happened to correct her on a few facts about her own baseball team, and we hit it off immediately. When she learned of my love of sports, she invited us out to San Diego for three days. I went to two Padres games and sat in the owner's box. I even went into the locker room and met some of the players. Steve Garvey gave me a baseball autographed by the entire team!

I also had my picture taken with Goose Gossage! I even had my name in lights on the scoreboard! It was quite a trip. One I won't forget. Joan was an incredibly generous and compassionate person, as she demonstrated many times over the years. During the floods in Grand Forks, North Dakota in 1997, I knew that the anonymous donor of millions of dollars for the flood relief effort whom they dubbed "The Angel" was Joan Kroc herself.

THREE

Adulthood:
Living with Cerebral Palsy

I SPENT THE SUMMER after graduation at the Courage Center in Minneapolis learning various things and partying a bit too. (For anyone who's interested, I like Dr. McGullicuddy's Menthol Mint Schnapps served very cold). A highlight of that summer was meeting Dennis Heaphy, another quadriplegic. Dennis and I had long talks together that summer and became best friends. Dennis and I understood each other in a way that was truly special. No one else, no matter how empathetic they are, could appreciate what it was like greeting the world daily with the challenges we both faced.

The following year in 1987, Dennis invited me to visit him in Boston where he lived. That trip to Boston stands out as my favorite because of the opportunity to connect with him.

I have learned that travel is not too difficult for me. I discovered I could get around pretty well with my portable wheelchair which folds up for storage on planes. Traveling is an adventure, and I really enjoy seeing new places. Not to say that I am spoiled or anything, but I am always the one who gets to pick where to go on the family trips.

In 1987, I also went to Disney World and Cape Canaveral.

I liked Epcot the best and had a great time. Everyone was very nice, and since I was in a wheelchair I didn't have to wait in line! At Cape Canaveral, I got a private tour of the site. I love to fly and I would like to ride in a space ship someday. That was a special memory.

In June of 1994, I took another trip with my family to Iceland to attend a wedding of some friends. I got a unique perspective of the culture because we stayed in our friends' home. For some time, I had been dreaming of a house, and I was shocked to realize when I saw our friends' home that it was the same one that I had been dreaming about. Iceland was awesome. I saw glaciers, and it stayed light almost twenty-four hours. The people in Iceland were very nice and handled my disability well. I found Iceland much more handicapped accessible than England had been.

In 1996 we took a trip to visit friends in Montana. We packed up the van and pulled a camper. They live in Kalispell, which is the southern base of Glacier National Park. The night we arrived it snowed twelve inches. This storm caused flooding and the closure of all the roads in the park. Our plans to explore Glacier National Park had to be changed. We had three days to kill before meeting up with the Landstrom's. We decided to explore the Canadian Rockies and Banff. What a great decision! The scenery was spectacular, with majestic mountains and the crystal clear waters of Lake Louise. While there, we stayed in a campground for people with disabilities and slept in a camper my parents had. One feature I remember was a special shower for people with disabilities. Most national parks don't have showers like this nor are the accommodations as nice. I also remember the numerous elk wandering around, along with the tame gophers and squirrels.

We found a guidebook in Banff highlighting handicapped accessible trails. We decided to explore one of them only to find out that the last twenty yards of the two-mile trail was not accessible. So after the two-mile hike, I could not reach the end or see the spectacular water falls. We were not very pleased with this result. However, the pancake breakfast the next morning and the gondola ride that afternoon made up for what I missed at the end of the trail.

In 1998, I went to British Columbia with my family to a place called Salt Spring Island. We had some friends that owned a treatment center in England. They had two homes, one in British Columbia and one in Arizona. British Columbia is absolutely beautiful, with mountains, lots of pine trees, and the water. It is often foggy and cool though. A whale-watching expedition was the highlight of that trip. We saw a pod of ten whales swimming together next to the boat. They were huge and very beautiful.

In 2001, I traveled with my family to Los Angeles to visit a cousin who lives there. My favorite sites were the Getty Museum, which had interesting art, and the Hollywood Walk of Stars. Unfortunately, I missed seeing anyone famous on that trip but was able to go to a Dodgers game. I also joined my family in St. Louis for a Grimm family wedding. We visited a Budweiser plant and saw how beer is made. We saw the huge Clydesdale horses, the famous mascots of the Anheuser-Busch Company. And of course, we got in a Cardinals baseball game.

Not all of my trips were so uplifting, however. I think all of us remember where we were when the planes hit the World Trade Center. My caregiver Rietta had just put me in my shower chair in the bathroom that morning on September 11, 2001. As usual, we had the TV on when we heard the news. Rietta ran out into the living room to see what had happened and then hurried back to tell me. I was so saddened by this event. I was also very concerned about Dennis and his family, who live in New York; and so I had one of my caregivers call him to find out if his brothers were okay. Fortunately, his brother who is a New York policeman came through this horrible ordeal safely. His other brother, who worked in a building next door, saw body parts flying from the Towers. It was very gross. Thousands of travelers were stranded by the shutdown of air traffic following the attack. My parents were in Nova Scotia at the time, and it took them about three or four days to return to Minnesota. My sister Mary was in Kansas City and couldn't fly home, so her husband at the time drove over 400 miles to go get her. This event is one of the key memories of my life.

In May 2002, my family went to New York to visit Dennis and his family. We stayed at an awesome hotel, the Doubletree in Times Square that Dennis' brother, the police officer, had arranged for us. It was shortly after 9/11, and New Yorkers were very willing to do favors for the cops, many of whom had so bravely risked their lives in that tragedy. We went to the site of the World Trade Center where I was moved to the front of a block-long line. I cried when I saw the cavity where the buildings had been. Workmen were still removing debris. Sadness was everywhere.

It was a busy week for us trying to see as much as possible. We went to the top of the Empire State building and toured the USS Intrepid Aircraft Carrier and Museum as well as the Rockefeller Center. (We didn't see the "Today Show" because we were always up so late that we couldn't rise before the sun.) We also went on a boat ride around the harbor and Statue of Liberty, walked to Central Park, and saw the Minnesota Twins play at Yankee Stadium. We covered a lot of territory during that week.

We also visited a fire station that had lost fifteen of their fellow firefighters. I told them they all deserved a medal for their bravery. It was a very emotional experience for everyone. I am reminded of that trip daily when I see New York on television and when I look at the hats I was given from both the New York Police and Fire Departments, which hang on a wall in my bedroom. Bin Laden should burn up like the victims of that horrible tragedy. It was a very good trip but I wouldn't want to live there.

After I graduated from high school, I had told my parents I wanted two things: to live independently and to have sex. The apartment happened first.

In 1989 my best friend Kyle and I moved in together at the Bungalow Apartments. Kyle was my caregiver. It seemed like a good idea but living together didn't work out very well. Kyle did not take very good care of things. Shortly after this, my good friend Jim Kelly found my next roommate Alicia. She was very cute. We lived together about ten months. I also lived with my sister Mary for about a year there. In total, I lived in the Bungalow Apartments for four years.

In 1992, I moved in with a caregiver and her family. It was a big adjustment for me and for them too. They had two sons who were cool and we had fun together. After two years it became too difficult for me to live there, and I moved back to live with my parents.

In those prior years, I was gradually finding that although I wanted independence I could never be alone. I feel most vulnerable when I am lying down. I often need assistance in the middle of the night to help with bodily functions, turning me to avoid bedsores, administering medication, and other things. So whom I lived with was hugely important. As a result I have fired several caregivers for not being attentive. I also could never have privacy, something that sometimes frustrates me.

When I left my caregiver's home in 1994, I went to back to live with my family for several years. Then in 1997, I moved into the Mary T. Home, an apartment complex for people with disabilities. I had two wonderful caregivers there, who I may have fallen in love with. They were very good to me. I also met a man who was a paraplegic and we starting hanging around together. Later, when I moved out of the Mary T. apartments into a house, I asked the two caregivers I liked so much to work for me. They agreed to do so. I also offered to have my friend come live with me in a spare room. We lived together for a total of four years. Unfortunately, he was subject to fits of anger and became jealous when my caregivers would pay attention to me. We also got drunk too much together. He was my good friend but he used me, and eventually, I had to kick him out. Now, looking back, I don't know why I didn't do it sooner. When I told him to move out, he didn't speak to me for a long time. (Recently, however, we did start to communicate again.) We had a deep relationship, but I was hurt by the way he treated others and me. Everyone who lives or works under one roof has to get along together, or it is not a sustainable situation.

I get used to people staring at me thinking that I am some sort of a freak. However, every once in a while, for whatever reason, I react with anger. There is one particular instance that endures.

One night my sister, Mary, and I went to the Porter House (the local restaurant and bar in Center City) with a bunch of friends. Mary tells the story best as I was too emotionally involved. These are her words: "James was sitting at the end of the booth and was staring directly at an older man across the room and had his tongue out with an awful sneer on his face. James spelled that he didn't like the man staring at him and told me to tell him to f___ off. Of course, I was not going to say that and I was not going to battle the crowd to get to where this man was sitting. I told Jim to ignore him and get his tongue back in his mouth, otherwise I would turn him around and he would have to stare at the wall. James clearly was not happy and kept sneering and scowling at the man. A few minutes later I turned around to find this old codger sitting right next to me in the booth and to find Jim's eyes open in surprise."

My sister Mary continued the story, "The man immediately apologized for staring and explained that he had been fascinated watching us throughout the night. He asked about our relationship. I told him that I was Jim's sister. He was amazed at how many people at the bar knew James and included him in their interactions and conversations. He said that if there was another Mother Teresa in the world that I would be the one. I was really flattered by that compliment. When recalling the story with James, he said that he felt real small after the man left because he assumed that the man was staring at him for reasons other than simple curiosity and fascination."

While I hate it when adults stare at me, it is quite another story when it comes to children. I remember the time I went to the flea market with Mom and my sister Mary. While we were walking about I saw this cute little boy peeking around his mother's side and staring at me. Just as I got Mary's attention and pointed him out to her, the little boy said to his mother quite loudly, "Mom, look at that big puppet!" Now to him I was a giant marionette! While his mother recoiled with embarrassment and came up to apologize I spelled for my mom to explain to the little boy what was wrong with me and how I communicated. Upon hearing this, the child wanted to speak to me directly. It took me some time before I got used to the staring of others but I am now comfortable with it.

FOUR

Home Sweet Home

IN 2000, MY FAMILY, in conjunction with a service in the Twin Cites called Life by Design, Inc., purchased a house in which I now live. This was a major step forward in my struggle for independence. Life by Design is an agency that provides supported living services to people with disabilities. The owners, Beth Hawkins and Linda Zeine, are great people. The essence of Life by Design is self-determination. It is their philosophy that people like me should be able to live on their own, not in a group home. Life by Design now owns ten homes in the Twin Cities. In addition to people like me who live on their own, Life by Design offers SLS (supported living services, serving clients in their own home) and In-Home Services (serving clients in their family home.). I have a great staff of caregivers through Life by Design who I can hire and fire at will, and I have been very happy with this agency. Living on my own is difficult, but I can still take care of my business. I love living in my own house. It's important to me that after I am no longer here that this house remain a home for people with disabilities.

It took six months to get the house ready for me. We had to make a ramp for the wheelchair and remodel the bathroom to make it handicapped accessible. We also added a bright and comfortable four-season porch and a deck. When we were done, we threw an open house and about 150 people stopped by to see it and celebrate with us. Unfortunately, not everyone was happy to have a person with disabilities move into the neighborhood. A neighbor came to the open house with a note saying, "People like him shouldn't live here." I wish she could have heard what I was thinking. It wasn't very nice.

As much as possible, my caregivers strive to give me control over the events in the house. For example, when the phone rings, my caregivers will answer it by saying "This is Jim." They will then hold it to my ear so I can hear the person. I stick my tongue out when the person on the line is done. Then they spell with me my reply and speak this back to the caller in first person, such as "I want to see Bob." Using this convention, it is as though I am speaking rather than having someone translate my thoughts or speak for me.

I have a keen sense of time. There is a rhythm to my day. I often know when it's time for my medicines without looking at a watch or clock. I will remind my caregivers, even though they likely know it's time for my medication since it's part of our daily routine. I sometimes feel I am a pain in the butt. At the same time it frustrates me when they are tardy, and I'm unable to get their attention when they are in another room.

My personal care attendants are a very important part of my life and have a special place in my heart. They help me live as normal a life as possible. They end up being a regular fixture in my life because I need them with me twenty-four hours a day. They are my friends, nurses, partners in crime and fantasies, personal counselors, drivers, secretaries, my uppers and downers, my enemies, pains in my ass, thorns in my side, my drill sergeants, bitches or bastards—just to provide a few affectionate descriptions. They have also been my confidants. However, I've made mistakes which taught me the lessons that not everyone can hold a confidence. At times it has ended up badly for me and I have been bitten in the ass. But there have always been a few special caregivers and friends whom I have been able to trust. There is no need to mention names as they know who they are.

I have had some very bad caregivers and they likewise know who they are. Again, there's no need to mention names. I can tell right away when I first meet them whether they will be both caring and well trained. My own intuition that allows me to discern and I am around 97% on target.

I call Kim my Angel because she has the habit of giving me angels when I have been sick and hospitalized. She has had a difficult life. We have had lots of fun together. She has accompanied me to the Tom Petty and Lynard Skynard concerts. I am blessed to know her and be her friend.

Jenny was a twin whose brother had cerebral palsy, which resulted from almost drowning when he was a young child. We were comfortable with one another from the moment we met. She worked so well with me because she had the experience of her brother's cerebral palsy. I fell in love with Jenny because she understood me so well and because she was beautiful.

I called Susie "Smiley" because she was always smiling at me. We are good friends, always there for one another. I could always trust her. She never told anyone the things I entrusted with her. She has been the most patient and most trusted caregiver that I have ever had. We can go without seeing or talking to one another for months and never skip a beat.

I can say anything to Rietta. She has always been a great advocate for me, knowing when to speak and when to be quiet on my behalf. Next to my sister Mary, she is and always will be my best friend and one of the best personal care attendants that I've been blessed to have. She allows me to be myself, always listens, and never judges. Rather than going to my family she allows me to make my own decisions, which in these latter years has been very important to me. I confide in her on personal and emotional matters when it would be awkward to go to my family. She is very frank and honest with me when she needs to be and that suits me just fine.

Amber and I will be very good friends forever. We hit it off immediately. The minute I saw her I knew I was in love with her. It feels awkward to have a twenty-one year old girl as a friend but I don't care. She is very attractive, being blessed with a great body, mind, personality, face, and above all beautiful eyes. She is my sweetheart. If life had been different I would like to have been more that just "friends" with her. But life has many different paths, and ours did not converge. When she is not with me there is an empty space and feeling in my life. She is one of the prettiest people I know. She is amazingly unaware of her own beauty.

Tammy is my personal nurse and another confidant. She doesn't like bull shit and gets to the point immediately. This is refreshing because it is not a common character trait these days. She says it like it is. We are the best of friends. I expect and hope that she will be in my life forever.

Amanda is like a little sister to me. She is a personal care assistant who takes me to my appointments and works with hospice. She is a very caring person who is always there for me, and who also speaks her mind on my behalf. Her own personal health challenges over the past two years have made her empathetic to my difficulties.

When I first met Chelsey I knew immediately we would be friends forever. Chelsey and I came into each others lives for a reason, both of us acknowledging that we are not quite sure why except that are we very good to and for each other. Chelsey has expanded my spiritual life greatly. We have gone to many spiritual events. We often talk about God and how He has touched each of us in so many ways, and how important He is in our lives. She has become part of my world and I pray that she never leaves it. She brightens the room with her big smile and bright blue eyes and her inquisitive and loving spirit, which allows her to take interest in anyone who crosses her path. She is the most beautiful person I know both inside and out. I would do anything for her! I believe that she feels the same about me. We listen to each other and support each other giving advice and not making judgment.

Chris is my friend. We are a great team together. I must say that he is probably the most patient of all my aides. He is always available to fill in or sub. I don't know how he does it. If he is not working at one of his other two jobs he is busy with a filming project.

I have always liked animals and grew up with pets. When I was a child, we had a cat named Snowball, a white cat who adopted my family, and we grew up together. I'm allergic to most cats, but wasn't to her. After I started living on my own, I wanted the companionship of a dog and so I got Sadie, an Eskipoo. Sadie knew I was her master, and we went everywhere together. If I leaned down in my wheelchair and put my face close to her, she would lick my face enthusiastically, covering me with dog kisses. I had her for fourteen years and just put her down a couple years ago. Making this decision was one of the hardest decisions of my life. However, her sight and hearing were declining, and she couldn't control her bladder. It was time. Sadly, I know I will never find another Sadie. I think about her every day.

Nikki is my best little friend. Also my little bug! At six pounds, she has a bark ten times her size and energy enough to match a sled of dogs. She came into my life when she was six years old. She became a mother of six litters of puppies. Her poor little body needs a break! She is quite the cuddle bug with my aides, but not really me. However, she lets my aides know when I need anything and stays close by. She doesn't cuddle with me because I think she is frightened by my spasms, but she will lie on my lap when I am inclined in my chair. My aides say that at night, if I make any movement or noise, she immediately alerts them. She is very needy but I believe that comes from growing up in a puppy mill where she had to fight for attention. She loves other dogs and thinks that they should love her in return. I don't know anyone who doesn't love her once they get used to her pawing at them for attention.

If you visit my house, you'll see many telltale signs that I'm a Vikings fan, such as a purple throw in the living room and a Vikings flag hanging outside. For many years, I had season tickets for the Minnesota Vikings and the Timberwolves. I love to watch the Vikings play. I took a road trip to their training camp in 2003, where I met head coach Mike Tice and quarterback Duante Culpepper. I got my picture taken with them. I've also attended many Twins games. Another highlight for me was seeing the Twins play in the 1991 World Series. In addition to pro sports, I also have season tickets for the University of Minnesota Gophers football team since 2002 and have loyally attended their games over the years.

I have traveled to several baseball stadiums: Wrigley Field in Chicago (right behind home plate), Busch Stadium in St. Louis, Yankee Stadium in New York (ten rows from home plate), Dodger Stadium in Los Angeles, Petco Park in San Diego, and Fenway Park in Boston. I have a collection on my living room wall of fourteen baseballs from different stadiums, including one that Steve Garvey gave me with the signatures of all the Padres players. Another is from the 2002 National League playoffs.

My birthday is February 1st, which often falls about the same time as the Super Bowl, a great reason to party. One year I overdid it a bit, and had five or six shots at a bar. Boy was Mom pissed when she came to drive me home! Another memorable birthday was my thirtieth birthday. We hosted about sixty people poolside at a Radisson Hotel. About fifteen people toasted me. One person wrote me a funny letter. I had a great time. I remember my Aunt Carol and my caregiver Sue told jokes all night long. I had a blast. I didn't go to bed until four in the morning.

I did try taking some college level courses. In the late eighties, I took three accounting classes at Pine City College. However, I got bored with them, and so did not pursue a college degree. Later, in 1997, I took a psychology class at Cambridge Community College and learned a lot. The brain is interesting. I seem to need adventure and challenge in my life though. I like sports, motorcycles, girls, and loud rock music. I'm a typical guy in many respects.

I briefly tried working for about ten months at a non-profit called RISE that employs people with disabilities. I used a switch by my foot to shred paper and documents. I shredded a lot of paper during those ten months. The job was very boring unfortunately. It's frustrating to know what I'm truly capable of, but restricted from doing at most jobs because of my physical limitations.

I have attended over forty concerts. At the risk of boring the reader, here they are: Alabama (6 times), Aerosmith (4 times), Luther Allison, Allman Brothers, AC/DC, Bon Jovi, Boston, BB King (3 times), Black Crows, Bee Gees, John

Cougar (2 times), Robert Cray, Shaun Cassidy (my first concert but don't tell anybody), Eric Clapton (2 times), Doobie Brothers, Eagles, Buddy Guy (2 times), Guns and Roses, John Lee Hooker, Elton John, Kiss, Lynrd Skynyrd, Johnny Lang, Metallica, Van Morrison, John Mayall (3 times), Paul McCartney, Tom Petty, Pink Floyd (my best concert ever), Bob Seger, Santana, Bruce Springsteen, U2, Van Halen, and War (and others that I have probably forgotten.) As you can see, I love music. In 1992, I had the opportunity to go backstage and greet Eric Clapton. It was very neat. He is a nice guy. I love his music. My older brother John claims the moment I met Eric Clapton, I met God. Another concert that stands out and was probably my favorite was seeing Pink Floyd in 1994. I saw the concert with my brother and sister, and we were ten feet from the stage! It was the best concert I have ever been to. I have the concert on DVD and replay it often. My favorite moment was when they played "I Wish You Were Here." Although I may not have been able to dance in the aisles, I was definitely rockin' inside.

Not all the good memories at those concerts were related to music. I still laugh when I think of the time I looked down from the balcony at an Aerosmith concert and saw a girl in a miniskirt below obviously unaware she had a long line of toilet paper sticking out of her butt like a tail. I remember I was pretty blissful the time Mary and I were on our way to see War at the Caboose Bar in Minneapolis. (I will not provide any incriminating details for this occasion.)

In Minnesota, the State Fair is the highlight event of summer. I have been to it several times over the years to see concerts and eat food that isn't part of my usual routine, such as gyros and cheese curds. My favorite State Fair memory was seeing Lynrd Skynyrd in concert with my sister Mary.

Although rock and roll is my favorite, I also like other music. In 1998, Mary and I went to Duluth to the Bayfront Blues festival to see BB King and other great musicians.

I like things that are fast and wild. I like to ride motor-cycles and have many Harley Davidson t-shirts. You can find many photos of me grinning with friends next to a shiny hot bike. I feel a connection with wildlife. In my house, images of wolves and bears appear in pictures and statues.

FIVE

Close Encounters

OVER THE YEARS, I have dealt with many challenging medical issues. In 1998, I had a Baclofen pump inserted surgically into my abdomen. I had read about it in a newspaper. It intrigued me because I had suffered my whole life with ongoing muscle spasms, and my legs were very stiff. This pump delivers medicine to my lower extremities on a regular basis to help stop muscle spasms. I felt immediate relief after it was inserted. Every three months, I go into the hospital to get it refilled. It truly has been a godsend.

In 1999, I tried Botox injections into my arms to relax these muscles. Unfortunately about three months after the third injection, I felt some discomfort in my chest and found I had contracted pneumonia. Apparently, the Botox injections paralyzed the muscles in my throat, which caused me to ingest food into my lungs. I probably drank too much too. I ended up catching pneumonia four times over the course of four years. If I had to do it over again, I wouldn't have gotten the Botox injections.

When you are a quadriplegic, your wheelchair becomes almost an extension of your body. For me, it is a source of great comfort and security. My new wheelchair, constructed by the New Brighton Specialty Clinic, was very expensive, but has a removable padded seat that was custom designed to mold to my body. I can even recline in it. I love my new wheelchair and could sleep in it. As it is, I spend all my waking time comfortably resting there. Able-bodied people may not realize this, but it is even possible to have sex in a wheelchair (I'll leave that to your imagination.). It also has a clicker near my left foot that I use to get my caregiver's attention, so I feel more in control in my wheelchair than I do lying down in bed. Rather than resenting the wheelchair, it has become my friend.

The year 2003 was tough. My family was on vacation that summer at a resort in Inger, Minnesota. Every year, we rent the entire resort for a week and about thirty relatives and friends come up to enjoy a lazy week together. One day, I swallowed some food which then entered my windpipe and went into my lungs, and I contracted aspiration pneumonia. I didn't realize how serious it was though, and we chose to drive back to Mercy Hospital which was about four hours away. I was very scared. I felt a great tightness in my chest. I nearly died. This was the second time that I came close to death. Most people have not experienced the possible end of their life even once, let alone twice. Rather than making me feel afraid of dying however, I am at peace with it.

The final bout with pneumonia led to my having a tracheotomy July 2, 2003. Not being able to breathe on one's own and the hassles of living with a trachea really suck sometimes. It creates inconveniences and gets me down at times. I had to change my life because it slowed me down a bit, and I couldn't do the things I like, such as swimming, eating, and drinking. (In chapter eight, I will describe what I call "The Miracle of the Trach Removal.")

In addition to the trach, I also have a feeding tube, which

is inserted in my abdomen through an incision. It delivers liquid medicine, water, nutrients, and crushed pills into my stomach and large intestine. Every three months it is replaced. My caregivers use a large syringe to administer these things. I take a psychotropic drug as part of my routine, and my caregivers will show me the bottle before crushing the pill and inserting it into the tube, a standard protocol for vulnerable adults.

I enjoy food and miss not being able to eat regular meals. Occasionally, one of my family members will feed me small amounts. My current favorites are cheese and eggs, pancakes with peanut butter, lamb, pot roast, and potatoes. When you don't eat food very often, you relish the taste more. There is always the danger of the food going down my windpipe, possibly causing pneumonia and choking. So it is a careful procedure, and that is why only my family feeds me. Because I have had repeated bouts of pneumonia, the time was coming when I might not be able to eat food any more. Not eating isn't too enjoyable to think about. It really sucks that I decided not to eat. I also miss an occasional drink.

From what I have already described in previous pages the reader should be able to conclude that, despite my physical handicaps, I also have a normal range of feelings: *frustration* with the failure of technology to help me; *anger* with some of my aides; *love* of and the *excitement* for sports, motorcycles and travel; *sorrow and sadness* while viewing the destruction of the World Trade Center; the *deep grief* at the loss of Sadie; and the genuine *fear* associated with the two encounters with my mortality. As I wrote in my journal, "I saw the gates of heaven when I was in the hospital but it wasn't my time."

After my close experience with death in 2003, the two years after had been the hardest of my life principally because of the rapid deterioration of my body. This in turn has magnified my fears and frustrations and given rise to my depression (about which I will write shortly). I wrote in my journal that the insertion of the trachea to assist me with my breathing: "changed my life. Sometimes I think about taking it out because I miss eating, drinking, and swimming. I wish I didn't have it—but if I didn't I wouldn't be here. On the other hand sometimes I wish I were dead because it sucks. I am glad when the holidays are over, because I don't have much fun sitting at the table watching everybody eat, some of them pigging out."

Of course, it infuriates me when people say they understand what I am going through. I wish they were in my shoes for a week—they would certainly learn a lot. For example, I hate the antibiotics I have to take when I have pneumonia and that lead to my loss of control over my bodily functions. It is no fun having diarrhea and not being able to do anything about it. Rather than being in my shoes then, I wish they were in my pants for a week.

I am sure that dealing with my body and its deterioration these past two years has been the leading cause of my depression. A long talk with my dad convinced me that what I was going through was quite "normal." It was okay to take the drugs being prescribed for me by my doctor. My counselor and friend, Paul Sherman, also helped me understand the value and positive points about taking this medication. Up to this point I was hesitant to take "any happy drug."

I wish I had known I was depressed. Then I was not very nice to my staff. I feel badly about that. I think everyone should see "Million Dollar Baby." The movie was a powerful one and the ending really hit my heart. I know the ending was controversial, but I feel that way sometimes. The movie confirmed my decision as to the DNR (do not resuscitate) order.

Let me tell you how I came to that decision. I have the best family in the world who are always there for me, especially during times of serious illness. But it is impossible for them to be there every single moment and to anticipate when I will need them the most. It is in that void or absence that I feel helpless and extremely anxious. The old refrain keeps repeating itself, "What if no one is there for me (as Bob was when I almost died)?"

When I was hospitalized after the vacation at Inger, I became very conscious of and sensitive to the rhythm, signals, and beeps of the machines to which I was hooked up. At the slightest change in the beat or volume I would panic, wondering if something were wrong. There was no one there to check on it. The same thing was true at the nursing home where I was transferred and getting used to the trachea. I wondered if I would die if something went wrong and no one was available at that precise moment to respond. Soon after, two important events occurred almost simultaneously: hospice care and the formulation of my Health Care Directive.

After I got my trach, my family and I had a meeting with Life by Design regarding the ability of their company to continue caring for me. Concerns arose because they did not employ a nurse for care services that I now needed. Life by Design was going to investigate options to determine what was possible. At that time their insurance did not cover the liability involved in caring for me in this new condition.

I myself brought up the option of removing my trach. My folks took me to see my pulmonologist, Dr. Nelson, to discuss the option. She said that if I chose to have my trach removed she predicted that I would have no more than six months to live. She then brought up the idea of having hospice care. Because I am terminal, she said, I would qualify and that would solve the problem of getting the appropriate level of nursing care. She already had a patient with MS in hospice care.

As a hospice patient now, I make my own choices. I have weekly visits by a personal nurse, my needs are more easily met, and I have 24-hour call for care. Moreover my family and caregivers are able to provide for my medical needs ordinarily done by a licensed nurse without liability concerns. They are my advocates in all my wants and needs. I am at peace because they are there for me and I know that they truly care.

Another benefit of hospice is that my personal nurse visits me weekly for a check-up. She is able to detect the earliest signs of pneumonia. If she hears crackling in the lungs she is able to prescribe antibiotics immediately. There is no need to go to the hospital for X-rays. Individuals with CP typically die either from pneumonia or heart failure. Once you get pneumonia you're likely to get it again and again until the body finally fails. I have had pneumonia six times in the past six months.

The trauma involved with being in the hospital and nursing home for two and half months prompted me after much thought to conclude that it was time to fill out a Health Care Directive. I simply did not have the strength or the will to go through a similar or worse traumatic experience. Initially I was afraid to bring it up wondering how my family and friends would respond. But my family was great especially Mary whom I trusted completely and knew would follow up on the decisions that I put in the directive. I appointed her my Health Care Agent.

A Health Care Directive is a document that tells medical personnel, family and friends what your wishes are in the event of a life-threatening situation. You determine what means are to be used to extend your life and under what conditions. I did not find it difficult to think about this, but others might. I am glad I did it because it gives me, my family, and caregivers peace of mind when we are facing the inevitable situation. My wishes are very clear. Everyone knows what they are. In the event that something should happen to me and I lose consciousness, I do not want to be resuscitated. My body could not take this again. Taking the time to complete a Health Care Directive is perhaps the ultimate statement you can make about control over your life.

I have had a great life and have had many great experiences, more than most people in this world would ever dream of. For this reason alone, if I died tomorrow, I would be okay because of the full life that I have lived and loved. I also believe that my body would not recover again from a severe case of pneumonia or whatever might send me back to the hospital. Even if it did, I know that my quality of life would have ended.

As you might imagine, Sand Lake raises unpleasant memories for me, and so I no longer join my family on the annual trek to the resort. In 2004, I got an infection in the incision for my Baclofen pump and my mom stayed with me for two weeks because I needed intravenous medicine. This is something my caregivers can not do, while Mom can because she is a nurse.

When I wrote the above, it was the winter of 2005. Despite all the adversity, 2005 had been a good year and wonderful things continued to happen: a Paul McCartney concert in October, a trip to Telemark, and seeing Lynrd Skynyrd again at the State Fair. I have lived a damn good life, but my time will come. I am at peace with that knowledge. I know God's purpose for me on this earth is to help people learn about disabilities. I will talk about my relationship with God in the closing chapter.

SIX

A Whole Person

———

PEOPLE WHO ARE ABLE-BODIED most often don't realize that those of us with disabilities have normal sexual drives just as they do. Just as I have feelings and thoughts like everyone else, so I have a sexual appetite similar to others with a need to satisfy it. People should not be surprised that I can be the recipient of love and affection while confined to a wheel chair.

On occasion, while being attended to by my mother, I have had to ask her to leave while visited by a close friend. Also on an occasional visit to a strip club my favorite dancers love to see me there and extend special welcomes.

My sister Mary and I have had good conversations about my sexual drive and my raging hormones especially after flirting with her female friends. The following is one event that I feel comfortable sharing with the reader.

My mom and dad decided to have a talk with me and suggested that I see a sex therapist. I agreed. After several sessions, the therapist suggested that I see a sex surrogate that he knew in Berkeley. Of course I jumped at the chance. I asked Mary to go along so that I would have someone to talk to about my experience rather than my folks.

On February 10, 1990 the Grimm Family flew to San Francisco for a week. We stayed at a Holiday Inn in downtown

San Francisco. Two days later, on the twelfth, the Grimm's rental car pulled up to a duplex in the city of Berkeley. This was the home and office of Cheryl Cohen, the sex surrogate that I would be spending four sessions with. As we walked up to the door of the house, Cheryl appeared. Both dad and I were amazed as our eyes set upon Cheryl. She was a tall leggy brunette with quite large breasts. I was in heaven when I saw her! There happened to be several steps up to the house so she called for her husband to come and help. Imagine the amazement when her husband appeared to help get me into the house! That was quite odd! He was a sex therapist as well, but not a surrogate.

Prior to the first session, she wanted to visit with all of us and learn more about how to communicate with me. My family explained how I spoke by going through the alphabet. We decided it would be best for me to ask her several questions and have her observe how I communicated. The first question I asked was, "How many men with cerebral palsy have you been with?" Cheryl said that she had been with quite a few to help them out with their sexual issues and with others, who for some reason or another could not bring themselves to have sex. After several other questions, my dad took me to the bedroom in the back.

While my dad was getting me situated, my mom and Mary were sitting in the waiting room laughing at all the books she had on ESO (Extended Sexual Orgasm) and the figurines scattered around displaying all the different sex positions. One could learn quite a bit just looking around the waiting room. A few minutes later my dad and family left to explore the Berkeley campus.

After a late lunch they came back to Cheryl's house to pick me up. It happened to be rush hour. We were at a stand still on the Bay Bridge trying to get back to San Francisco. Cars were on both sides of us. Little did anyone around us know what we had just done. My dad said, "Well son, what do you have to say for yourself?"

"If I was a woman, I'd never do that to a man!" I replied.

In unison, my family all said, "Jim got a blow job!" I just sat there and grinned, the biggest grin you have ever seen!

We happened to have a free day the next day so we drove to Carmel and Pebble Beach. What a place! I was certainly distracted from the beautiful scenery around me.

I met the sexual surrogate again on February 14th—Valentines Day! We proceeded with the same routine. They dropped me off at Cheryl's office and came back a few hours later. On our way back to the hotel that day we once again were at a dead stop in traffic on the Bay Bridge. Again my dad said, "Well James, how did everything go today?"

I spelled, "Mom and Dad, the only thing I will tell you is that everything works very well!"

Mary's response was, "This is not fair. It is Valentines Day and Jim is the only one that gets lucky!" Of course, I was grinning from ear to ear. It would have been a great scene in a movie! Little did anyone know what the Grimm family was up to and what kind of conversation was happening in the tan Taurus on the Bay Bridge.

Before leaving for home, I had two more sessions with Cheryl. At the end of the fourth session we were all sitting in the office. Cheryl happened to say that she thought it was the greatest thing that the whole family was involved in this experience for Jim. It was especially funny though, when the time came for Dad to pay the bill! If I remember correctly, she charged $80.00 per hour and after twelve hours the bill came to $960.00. To see my dad flip the bills out of his pocket and count out $960.00 for his son to have sex was quite a sight! It also seemed to be quite an experience for Cheryl as well!

Mary and I still have good conversations regarding sex and our experiences, but we won't go any further than that in this book!

We did have a few great road trips while there—going to the Muir Woods, visiting friends of Dad's, driving to the coast, eating great food, and spending time with the greatest people in the world: my family!

To this day, this trip is one of my favorite stories! Not many have had the experience that I had and then could share it with his family!

SEVEN

Family and Friends

I AM FORTUNATE to have a great family because many disabled people don't have one. I know I would not make it without my family. My family has always supported me in my wishes and come to my defense with others. When we were little, kids stared at me. John and Mary, my brother and sister, would say if they didn't stop staring they would beat them up. John and Mary have been so good to me. We get along very well, like friends. We don't experience the sibling rivalry other families face. Perhaps it is because we each have our unique role in the family. I don't get angry at my family very often, though I do remember a time when Mary was mimicking me. I didn't like it when someone made fun of me, and this set me off. I got very red in the face and tapped the clicker by my foot repeatedly to get her to stop. I had a scream boiling inside of me wanting to get out. Even though I couldn't speak, it was very obvious to everyone that I was upset!

John is four years older than me, and although we are not as close as Mary and I are, he has always been there if I need him, particularly when I wanted another male perspective. John is now an electrical engineer, married with two children, Morgan and Wesley. He is a great Dad. Mary is two years older than I and we are very close. She is very caring and always concerned for others' welfare. She is also great fun to be with and has a terrific sense of humor.

I have a good relationship with both my parents. I am probably a bit closer to my Mom. If it wasn't for her, I don't think I would be here, because she stayed with me at the hospital more than anyone else after my Sand Lake incident. It made me feel secure. Her background as a nurse had obviously been very beneficial. She is a caring, smart, and incredibly patient person. However, she is also strong and tenacious. I am so thankful to have had her support over the years as I confronted countless challenges to living a normal life.

My Dad is wise, and I go to him for advice on many things. Not too long ago, I was seriously depressed and wanted to die. I just didn't want to live any more. I was sick of my damn trach. It limits my life so much. I talked to Dad and my counselor Paul about my depression. Dad's response was "you have a right to be depressed." I am so glad he acknowledged and affirmed my feelings, rather than dismiss them, as other people might. He helped me get medical assistance to counteract the depression. I am now on Lexipro, and have found it helpful in managing my down times.

My dad has a wonderful sense of humor and is a great person. Sometimes though, because he is so intelligent, he has a hard time admitting he is wrong. It is easier to let things go than to try to defend an argument with him. You would be sitting there a long time! This has become a standing joke in our family.

My parents are very accepting people. They both let us be who we wanted to be as we were growing up. We were encouraged to try things, and they supported almost any activity we wanted to do. Even if we failed, they knew we would learn from the experience. And importantly, they were there to console us when things didn't go as hoped. Having this support enabled me to do many things that other people with Cerebral Palsy might be discouraged from trying. My life has been so much richer because it has been about finding creative ways to make things happen, rather than setting limits or making assumptions.

I have been fortunate to have many good friends in my life, several of whom I have stayed in touch with for decades. I have mentioned some of my friends earlier in this book. However, there are a few other people who have been important in my life, and I would be remiss if I did not mention them here.

Jay Nelson stands out as a life-long friend. Jay and I were neighbors as children, and over the years we have shared many experiences. One day, just for fun, we dressed up like Kiss and walked around town. Two guys in outrageous makeup, one of whom is in a wheelchair, definitely got us noticed! Another time, Jay and I brought a dog into church, took the elevator downstairs, and let him loose. We felt wickedly proud that no one knew it was us! Now as adults we go to a lot of games together and I was best man in his wedding. My affection for Jay extends to his wife Eileen, who I have a crush on. She's a very sweet person.

If you want a stand-up guy in your corner, John Flickie is the man. He was my protector. Children can sometimes be cruel to one another, and it takes courage to stand up to bullies. I remember a time a boy said I was dumb, and John told him if he didn't stop he would beat him up. I can take care of myself, but I still appreciate knowing someone is there to watch your back.

Missy was a friend in junior and senior high. She was

quieter than some of my other friends, but fun to be with, smart, and caring. We shared a lot. I was her confidante when she was going through a difficult time. We went to dances together. I had girls fighting over each other to dance with me! Regrettably, I have lost touch with Missy. I hope to reconnect with her some day.

I seemed to have formed more friendships with women than men over my life. I'm not sure why. Most of my friendships were on an individual basis rather than doing things in groups. Jenny, who I mentioned earlier in this book, was a very special friend. We were friends from first grade right through senior high. Jenny had a wonderful sense of humor, and one time she hid me from my aide. She was cute and wonderful, and I had a crush on her. I still see her once in awhile. Another friend all through school was Don Ertl. The last time I saw him was at his wedding a few years back. One time, when we were about sixteen, Don came to my family's cabin for a visit. He went for a run and got lost. When he didn't return, we got concerned and my uncle Mayo went out looking for him. Fortunately, he found his way back eventually. Don was smart and wise. He always treated me better than anyone else in my class.

Jonathon Dodge was another childhood friend and neighbor, who I am still in touch with. He was great fun. He was one year older than I, and he took me to our senior party. It was an overnight lock-in. We all had a blast. I know his family, also. His sister Cecelia, director of special education for the Hastings, Minnesota School District, invited me to give talks to her staff and students.

I met many other people through my medical events. Amy was my favorite staff person at the Courage Center and was a lot of fun. Jim Kelly was my speech therapist from high school whom I remain friends with today. Jim is a very good guy. He is a little strange but wonderful. Jim is a person to have adventures with. Jim took me to Sturgis, South Dakota to see the Harley motorcycle rally one year. Everyone was very nice there. Other times, we have headed over to St. Paul, Minnesota for fun times. No need to say more.

Dennis Heaphy, my buddy in New York who I met at the Courage Center, is my inspiration. People say I inspire them, but Dennis is someone I admire mightily. I was born as a quadriplegic. Dennis was able-bodied and lost it all in a diving accident. He had everything but his brain and voice taken from him, yet he continues to be upbeat and encouraging to others.

Another very important person in my life is Marty Stone. Marty is an engineer who used to be with Gillette Children's Hospital in Minneapolis. I met him though at Camp Courage where he helped feed me. I asked him to help me find ways to communicate, and he has tirelessly sought creative ways so that I could do so. My toe switches, head gear, the computer that I could type with Morse Code, all of which I mentioned earlier in this book, came from Marty's mind. He is very intelligent and creative and has worked tirelessly over the years to help me. I am truly indebted to him. Marty, I love you.

Another very dear and special friend is Paul who has been my counselor over the past twelve years. I sometimes feel that if I did not have Paul I would go nuts. He has been a stabilizing influence in my life. Besides giving me the opportunity to bitch (I tell him everything) he is my stabilizer, sounding board, and the one who with my dad has helped steer me through my bouts of depression. I both want and value his opinion.

One of my caregivers, Lisa, is very special to me. She has been assisting me for thirteen years, and over that time we have grown very close. She can read my mind, and we often laugh together remembering a shared moment. She knows everything. There are no secrets between us. I can be as crazy as I want to be with her because we both love to have fun and she totally accepts me. I can be completely open with her. I wouldn't have made it this far without Lisa. I have asked certain people, including Lisa, if they would like to contribute to my book. Their comments appear in Part Two. Hopefully through their words, you can learn more about what it is like to be in my world.

EIGHT

The Miracle of the Trach Removal

The night of June 4, 2006

I am not scared because the trach sucks. I don't think I could live with the trach much longer. I would rather take the chance of this surgery than fight every day living with the trach. I have lots of friends and family who are supporting me on this. Many came to visit or called to wish me well today. I appreciate everyone's thoughts and prayers as I go into surgery* tomorrow.

---

*Editor's Note:
This chapter describes the laryngectomy which Jim underwent. The operation consists of the surgical removal of the larynx and separation of the airway from the mouth, nose, and esophagus. The laryngectomee breathes through an opening, a stoma, in the neck. The larynx is located slightly below the point where the throat divides into the esophagus, which takes food to the stomach, and the trachea (windpipe), which takes air to the lungs. Because of its location, the larynx plays a critical role in normal breathing, swallowing, and speaking. Within the larynx, vocal folds (often called vocal cords) vibrate as air is exhaled past, thus creating speech. The epiglottis protects the trachea, making sure that only air gets into the lungs. When the larynx is removed, these functions are lost. Once the larynx is removed, air can no longer flow into the lungs. During this operation, the surgeon removes the larynx through

Thoughts after surgery

I thought the procedure was going to be worse that it really was. I thank the Lord for helping me get through. I thank my Life by Design staff for helping out by fulfilling their shifts up at the hospital. I couldn't have done it without my wonderful family: They are awesome! I have such great doctors and nurses at Mercy Hospital. When I got my trach, it was such a pain in the butt. Sometimes I wanted to die. I believe God made me for a reason. I didn't know the truth. I had second thoughts about God during my deepest and darkest times of depression, but once again He came through. His will gave me the courage to try new technology and surgery to help improve the quality of my life.

I know we are all different because God wouldn't make each of us the same. That would be scary. Life would be very dull. We would not be fun at all because we would fight all the time.

We all need different challenges in our lives to help us grow and thrive to move on. My body happens to be my main challenge. Something very few people can understand. With constant and continual challenges come constant and continual changes and personal miracles. Starting as a child

---

an incision in the neck. The surgeon also performs a tracheotomy. He makes an artificial opening called a stoma in the front of the neck. The upper portion of the trachea is brought to the stoma and secured, making a permanent alternate way for air to get to the lungs. The connection between the throat and the esophagus is not normally affected, so after healing, the person whose larynx has been removed (called the laryngectomee) can eat normally. However, normal speech is no longer possible. Several alternate means of vocal communication can be learned with the help of a speech pathologist.)

who could not communicate with his world, along comes communication with my tongue using the alphabet. My difficult hard spasms were calmed by the Baclofen Pump. Tight arm spasms were relaxed by Botox injections into my arms which unfortunately led to five bouts of aspiration pneumonia. My fifth pneumonia was relieved and my life saved by my trach. BUT with this came a loss of my quality of life, having to be deep suctioned and constantly living with fear of a mucus plug and suffocating, not to mention all the pressure on my staff with new and complicated responsibilities. Not being able to travel easily due to all the equipment and oxygen apparatus, as well as going through depression and a loss of will to live. But then once again, God blesses me with a great medical staff taking care of my needs and new technology to increase my quality of life. My laryngectomy was extremely successful. I feel like I have a big part of my life back. I no longer need to worry about aspiration pneumonia and can eat and drink when ever and what ever I want. No more hauling oxygen stuff around. My larynx was removed so I can never vocalize but I communicate in my own way and in my own words. I always have and always will.

My first real drink of water after my surgery came on July 2, 2006 when I was on South Center Lake in my parent's pontoon along with my mom, dad and sister Mary. I was in heaven after my first gulp of cool water. Isn't it amazing how something as simple as drinking water could elicit such joy? My first meal was steak. Once again, I was in heaven.

I am so glad I had the surgery because I can enjoy food again. When I had my surgery I was nervous that I wouldn't be able to eat, however a miracle happened and I was able to enjoy my favorite family cooked meals. The meals I enjoy again are omelet's, steak, spaghetti, lamb roast, walleye, prime rib, and for dessert a shot of Dr. McGullicuddy's schnapps. My staff was very excited for me to finally eat again. When I had my first meal, it was great. I was so scared that I wouldn't be able to swallow the first bite of food. Not to worry any longer about choking was a new, exciting, and unexpected feeling. I breathe only through my stoma, not my mouth. Anything that goes in my mouth can now only go to my stomach. I can't choke! Period! What a great but strange sensation. At times, I forget that I can't choke and will again get all uptight.

Now that I am more comfortable with eating again, I am having friends over for dinner quite often and going out to eat on a regular basis. My life is again full with activities. I must say that the quality of my life is back again.

The end of July 2006, I attended my twenty-year class reunion. I had such a blast. It was especially great due to the fact that I didn't have to worry about my trach. No one even knew I had a stoma! It was so much fun seeing everyone and telling them of my life and experiences the last twenty years. If nothing else, my trach has been a great story. All are especially excited to get a copy of this book.

I was reunited with long lost friends and heartthrobs. They are all doing well and heartthrobs are even sexier! I plan on having a bunch of them over for a famous "Grimm Party" in 2007!

I also attended the Duluth Air Show, which I believe all should experience. What a blast! I even made it through seven hours of 95 degree and sunny weather sitting on an airstrip. Very much worthwhile especially seeing the Stealth Bomber, the B-52 bomber, and the Thunderbirds speeding 500 feet above your head. You can feel the power throughout your body!

My concert list is continuing to grow. Mary and I went to see Eric Clapton for my third time and I just bought tickets to see Bob Seeger for my second time! I also have had the privilege to see Colin Powell at the Northrop Auditorium as part of a Leadership Series presentation. What a great human being he is! It was amazing to hear what he said about his opposing views of the current administration and the state of the world.

I am also taking adult education classes covering such topics as conflict resolution, community involvement, citizenship, and the war in Afghanistan and Iraq. And once again, football and basketball seasons are underway. I have Gopher football and Timberwolves season tickets again this year. I will enjoy them so much more! Not having the trach has given me a whole new enjoyment for things.

The Elevator

This is one of those stories that you hear about and are not sure if to laugh or feel bad for the people involved. My dad and I went to the much awaited Minnesota Gopher Football game against North Dakota Bison. As usual we left early hopefully to get lucky enough to snatch a decent handicapped parking spot near the dome. We ended up parking in the medical center ramp a few blocks north of the dome.

My dad pushed me into the elevator. He realized just then that he was not sure of what floor we parked on. He quickly leaned out of the elevator to check the floor number, thinking that his foot was in the door to prevent the elevator from closing. To his surprise —not mine because I was facing in—the door closed and the elevator started its way down. My poor dad was horrified. I had no idea of what was happening. I thought my dad was on the elevator with me.

He tried to stop the elevator by pushing the buttons but once the elevator is in motion there's no hope in stopping it with a measly button. My dad ran as fast as he could down the first flight of steps, the next, and then the next to the mezzanine level where he thought it would stop. No luck! The elevator continued to go to street level. During this time the elevator made two stops to load more people. My dad obviously missed each one. When the people started trying to talk to me, and I heard no response from my dad, I knew something strange was going on. It finally dawned on me that my dad was not there! By the time my dad made it down to the street level these people had pulled me out of the elevator and were trying to figure out what to do with me. My dad was terribly embarrassed but relieved to find me. I was thankful that my dad had not fallen down the steps when hurrying down due to his bad ankle and grateful of the kind people to stay with me. One of the gentlemen had a cell phone and was just about to call 911 when my dad showed up.

The Gophers won the game but did not deserve it, because the Bisons out played them the whole game!

Sometimes I feel like a failure. My damn body! Sometimes I really hate it. But if I had a normal functioning body I probably would have died years ago. I know I'd like the feeling of adrenaline rushes brought about by high speeds on a motorcycle and other risky situations along with consumption of large amounts of alcohol and crazy nights with luscious babes. My disabilities probably kept me alive. I wouldn't have had such a great life full of ups and downs if I had a normal functioning body.

Two more angels have come into my life since my trach surgery. They are Raven and Amy, my new caregivers. Both have impressively positive attitudes and are good caregivers. I have no concern about my needs when they are with me.

Raven has become a very good friend in an amazingly short period of time. She doesn't allow me to get down and depressed. When she senses me heading that direction she quickly halts it with her stories of inspiration along with her humor. She has given me the phrase, "You can't change your life story." Everyone has their own story and no one else can own it. Everyone has his or her tough times. We learn from each other. She always says to me that I can't sweat the small stuff and that God gives us only what he knows we can handle. She gives me strength and determination! I think that Amy and I were meant to meet each other at this time in our lives. We inspire each other. Amy is an inspiration to me because of her life story. She is one strong woman.

You can't change your life story, and *this* is mine.

God Has Blessed Me—
or Has He?

HAVING RECENTLY CELEBRATED my 40th birthday, I look back on my life and recognize that I have been blessed in many ways with family, friends, and many opportunities. I have done more in my short life span of forty years than most people ever will.

In school I was treated like everyone else and never left out of activities. I have traveled throughout the United States and many countries in Europe. One of my gifts is a great love for music and I have attended hundreds of concerts. Handicapped seating is always a plus at concerts and often the seats are front and center. Another of these gifts is my love of sport and again I have had hundreds of opportunities to attend games. I have season tickets for the Minnesota Vikings, Minnesota Gopher Football, and the Minnesota Timberwolves. Never a dull moment as I have been to many Minnesota Twins games also. The opportunity to own and live in my own home is one of my biggest blessings. Only about one percent of the people with disabilities in the world have that opportunity, and I am one of them. I feel that my greatest blessing is being able to breathe and to experience all the wonderful things that life has brought to me.

It is only a rare moment when I feel abandoned by God. The winter of 2004–2005 was one of them. Doubts about God's unconditional love for me made their appearance during these past two years when my body was failing me. I was very depressed and just wanted to die. I suppose it was only natural for these doubts to arise. When I think that I am cursed I am really only talking about my damn body with which I get frustrated. That is only natural, and the trach doesn't help matters.

On the other hand there is a positive side to having this trach because I have met so many people who have helped me and are special like the people involved in the hospice program. These include Bev Hood, my personal nurse who understands how I want to live and is one of my greatest advocates, Kathleen the Chaplain, Melissa, the physical therapist, and Teresa, the massage therapist.

If I were not disabled I believe that I might have died long ago dependent upon alcohol. Although I love the feelings that it induces, I am satisfied that it is no longer a part of my life as I am very glad to be alive. I would like to be on this planet and a part of the world community for five more years, both because I enjoy life and because I am treated like a normal person. I want to be remembered as an optimistic and caring person who did not let his disabilities get in the way of living life to its fullness in a manner that very few can boast. But I have always felt that God meant for me to be this way. I believe that I can help others—families and the disabled—to understand and accept the disabilities. I truly believe that I can inspire and help others see that disabled people can live normal lives.

And that is the principle reason for my autobiography!

(Above) My brother John,
sister Mary, Myrtle the turtle,
and me at Christmas 1968

(Right) My mother Esther
and me

(Below)
Damian McElrath
and me

(Above) What a smile!

(Right) My fourth-grade birthday party with friends

(Below) Me as Gene Simmons of KISS

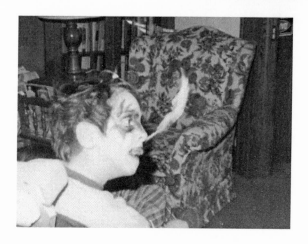

(Left) Mom and me visiting with Joan Kroc

(Below) Meeting Steve Garvey in San Diego Padres locker room

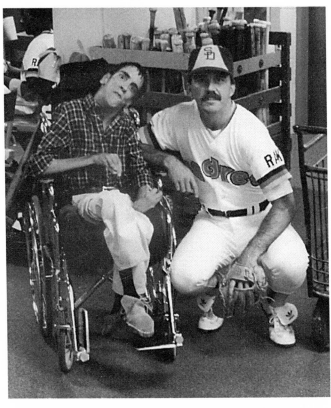

(Above) Visiting with Dennis Heaphy on Boston University Campus
(Below) Meeting students at a local elementary school

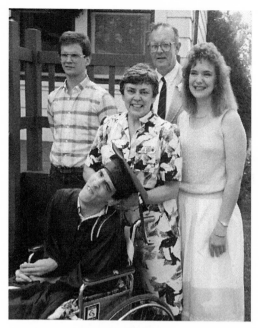

(Above) My high school graduation with my family
(Below) My brush with fame. Meeting Eric Clapton

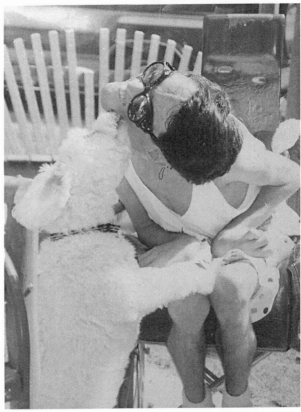

(Above) My best friend and sister Mary and me in Iceland
(Below) My other best friend, Sadie and me bonding!

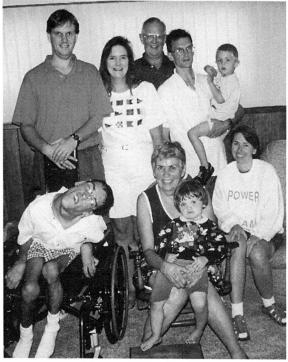

(Above) Visiting a fire station in New York May 2002
(Below) The Grimm family. Front row (left to right): Jim,
Esther (mother), Morgan (niece), Amy (sister-in-law). Back row
(left to right): Kent Brevik, Mary (sister) Gordy (father)
John (brother) and Wesley (nephew).

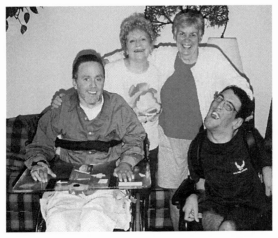

(Above) My friend Dennis,
me and our mothers

(Right) Chelsey and me

(Below) My caregiving crew

PART TWO

As Others See Me

As Others See Me

Parents, Esther and Gordy Grimm

How do we begin to write about forty years filled with love, heart aches, grief, happiness, hard work, frustration, doubt, challenges, letting go—but mainly understanding, patience and love?

We were both thirty-four years old when Jim was born. John was four years old and Mary about two. We were both in caring professions, a registered nurse and a Lutheran clergy, with helpful caring family, friends and neighbors—all of which helped us cope with the stress of uncertainly and exhaustion through the early years. We also believe that working with chemically dependant people and the AA philosophy helped us "Let Go, Let God" and take "One Day at a Time." These slogans are very needed in everyday life and "growing up" with a very physically disabled child.

We realized early on, when Jim was about three or four months old, that Jim was not developing his motor skills as he should. His non-verbal communication was always "right-on"—his sparkling eyes and smile. Our household has always been a busy one with family and friends coming and going. It became more so when we started Jim on

Doman Delacatto therapy at age one. Our friend and neighbor Irene became our volunteer coordinator and scheduled about sixty volunteers to "pattern" Jim four times a day. Jim then became a member of a "caring community" which has continued throughout his lifetime. Jim was very intuitive and did not appreciate the few volunteers that felt sorry for him by saying, "poor Jim;" he then continued therapy at Curative Workshop (Courage Center) and then Michael Dowling with many of the same volunteers driving him to either of these facilities. He always seemed to enjoy meeting all these individuals, whether they were teachers, students, therapists or other rehab staff.

When Jim was to start first grade, one of the teachers Mrs. Mitchell requested to have him in her class—which was a great beginning. Jim was a pioneer at the school as a mainstreamed severely physically disabled student. It was a challenge for the administration and faculty. They were very concerned, cooperative, supportive, and innovative. It benefited Jim, other students, administration, and teachers. Jim wrote about his communication but I would like to write about it in more detail. When he learned the alphabet in first grade his tongue became his communication. He learned to spell quickly, and we all learned short cuts. If the first letter of a word he selected started with "s," we would then say, "h, l, t, p"—then "a, e, i, o, u." If the first letter was "w" we would say "h" then prompts like "when, where, why, what, who or which." There are also other shortcuts. Through the years this seemed to be the best communication for Jim and for us. He has tried many switches through the years but due to his poor motor control, body positioning, and perfectionism they didn't work for him. His perfectionism showed up when he was on the computer. He would spend most of the time correcting his mistakes. He had what we called "antici-patory reflex." He would hit the switch too quickly making a mistake. Also when doing his homework, he would tell us to be neater.

Jim's school years were good. His classmates recognized he was a bright kid locked into his body. He was always blessed with very good one-on-one aids, such as Jan, Barb, Carol, and Teresa. In grades one through twelve, each of his aids were sensitive, respectful, loving, and let Jim do his work. They were the facilitators.

Jim liked to go to school dances starting in seventh grade. We would drive him over to school and soon he would tell us to "go," knowing that his friends would be with him. He did like the girls!

On sleepovers, he would have Jay, Don, Joel, and other friends over listening to music, talking sports and girls. One day, when he was about sixteen, he came home from school looking very distraught. We asked him what was wrong and he spelled, "This is very hard for me to ask my mother, but could you find someone for me to have sex with?" We real-ized this would be an on-going problem. He had a normal male sex drive but no way to satisfy it. So throughout his adulthood he has seen many counselors and sex therapists, which resulted in our going to Berkley, California to a sex surrogate and therapist. Living now as a semi-independent, he has found his own resources.

One of Jim's other pleasures was eating. We fed him by standing on the side of his wheel chair, holding his head with our left arm and feeding him with our right. He enjoyed prime rib, walleye, spaghetti, lasagna, cheesecake, carrot cake, and other foods. So when he got aspiration pneumonia and had a tracheotomy it was very difficult for him. He had the trach for about 3 years and in June 2006 he had surgery to separate the esophagus from the trachea (wind pipe) so he can now eat without the risk of choking.

John and Mary were always concerned about Jims' progress and well-being. They were very patient with him and us as parents. They understood we needed to spend more time with him because he was so physically dependant. They probably felt neglected or left out at times, but we tried our best. During John and Mary's teen years, we tried not to put too much "Jim sitting" or responsibilities on them so they would be come resentful. They included Jim in their conversations, activities, and continue to be very attentive, taking him to sport activities, concerts, and out to eat.

Jim never seemed to feel sorry for himself through childhood and most of his adulthood. When we would come home from Courage Center or Gillette Children's Hospital, he often would spell, "It could be worse." Some of the most difficult years were when he had his tracheotomy. He didn't eat because of the fear of aspiration, and he wasn't as socially active.

One of his goals was achieved when he moved into his house and was a client of Life by Design. It proved that he could live semi-independently and manage his home, money, and caregivers. We are very grateful to Life by Design and their staff for supporting Jim so he could live a fulfilling life.

And so the journey continues. We are thankful and amazed that Jim has been able to maintain his sanity and be positive (his vibrant personality) throughout his years of sever physical disability and being non-verbal.

Jim has a strong faith and believes that God has a purpose for him. Jim has been therapeutic to many people who have personal problems, such as with health, chemically dependant, or feeling sorry for ones self. He has accepted his disability and lives a full life which is a challenge for everyone. The Serenity Prayer has been very meaningful to him. This is the prayer:

> God grant me the serenity
> to accept the things I can not change;
> the courage to change the things I can;
> and the wisdom to know the difference.

Jim and our family could not have coped without the caring community. We are very thankful for family, friends, staff, and agencies that have helped us and other challenged individuals.

Jim is an inspiration to us. He has enriched our lives and we have known a deeper love which God has given us through a disabled son. He is God's gift.

Sister, Mary Grimm

I don't know where to start. When it comes to my brother, I could fill volumes so I will need to pick one focus—my brother and best friend. I've always told people that even though Jim is my brother, he is also my best friend. We have this bond that is like no other. We always have and always will.

As far back as I can remember, I wanted Jim happy and be sure that everything was fine with him. I've always said, "If Jim is okay, then I am okay!" I thought I had to be his entertainment coordinator, caretaker, and protector and still do to this day.

During the trips to the grandparents in Clear Lake, Iowa or in Willmar when we were little we'd lay in the back of the station wagon, and I'd and make up songs to sing to Jim. If

I wasn't singing, I'd tell stories; and I would go on for hours and hours. I don't recall ever stopping. Some would say that I still haven't stopped! I would even dance on the kitchen counters to make him laugh and smile. When Jim smiles, his eyes sparkle and he brightens your day, which in turn always brightens my day.

In 1986, I will never forget his first week at Courage Center and having to go through the adjustments of a new living situation and caregivers. As usual, in the beginning, Jim and the caregivers struggle trying to understand each other. I don't know if it was more difficult for him or me. I was so distraught that I convinced myself that I was going to quit college and dedicate my whole life to taking care of Jim, and then everything would be "okay." As it ended up he had a great experience, learned a lot and made many good friends and did just fine on his own!

I am known to most people as a chatterbox and will talk to most anyone very easily. Jim is a great listener, and I think when I am on a roll and start talking incessantly he at times probably checks out and doesn't even pay attention to me. But when I truly need someone to talk to, Jim has always been there. Whether it is a broken heart, bad day at work, or just being plain mad at someone or about something he comes through. He knows exactly what to spell to cheer me up. He is always the first person that I turn to in times of excitement and good news. If he is not along on one of my adventures I always find myself thinking, "I can't wait to tell Jim about this" or "I have to take Jim here!"—again appears the "event coordinator." I think it is he who has given me the ability to always find something good out of a bad situation or find "the silver lining" in everything. That perhaps has come from his positive view on life. He has always said that God has meant for him to be the way he his, and his job is to help inspire others and that there is a reason for everything.

He is also a chatterbox and I believe he could actually out do me in the world of conversation. By the time you read this you already know how he communicates and the process that we go through. This does take a great amount of patience for both parties, him in particular when we on the receiving end of his spelling and can't understand what he is trying to say. I believe my patience has also come from growing up and spending lots of time with him. I always find time for him no matter what the situation and will spend hours spelling with him.

I always need my "Jim fix." I rarely go a day without at least talking to him on the phone. Even when I was in college I'd call home to talk to him or write long rambling letters. My parents threatened once to cut the phone lines because of my big phone bill that they were paying (of course).

Activities and events are always more fun when Jim is involved. To many people he is perceived as "lots of work." When you take Jim anywhere you must plan on getting ready and leaving much earlier than normal. For all Vikings, Timberwolves, Twins, or Gopher games (all sports that Jim loves to go to), you must get there early to get available handicapped parking. Once you arrive, handicapped seating is always guaranteed to be some of the best—especially at concerts. I always joke with Jim and tell him that the only reason I take him places is that I can get pushed up to the front of the line and get the best seating available because of his disability. In actuality, I would not have had all the wonderful experiences in my life if Jim were not a part of it. You always seem to have more fun when Jim is involved because he takes more pleasure and great joy in them.

Jim is always busy, not wanting to stay home. Concerts

(well over 50 of them), sporting events, restaurants, a weekly dinner with family or a special friend, walks around Lake Calhoun, and now his new interest, air shows. He is always on the go and many of these times I was the coordinator. Like I stated before, if it wasn't for him, I would have never done so many fun things!

For both of us, being one of the Grimms also means that both James and I are very gregarious, so obviously we enjoy socializing, being in crowds, and partying. Many nights I had to push Jim home from the local bar, sneak in the door to turn off the intercom so mom and dad wouldn't hear us stumble and roll in the door. I would then get in trouble when the van was not in the driveway the next morning, which is a huge clue that we both probably had too much to drink. What really gave it away is when Jim was extremely thirsty in the morning! We always had and still have way too much fun when we are together.

Jim always has had a dog as a companion: Lassie, a rat terrier through high school, Sadie, an eskipoo for twelve years, and now Nikki a toy poodle. These dogs have definitely been "Jim's best friends." The animals are no different from me in terms of their dedication to his happiness. They were always there to cheer him up, and he always wanted to be sure that they had the best of everything. Sadie immediately bonded to him and never left his side. She was lost without Jim. In 1990 to 1991, James and I lived together in the Bungalows in Chisago City. On the weekends James would go home to stay with my parents. One night I asked him if Sadie could stay with me, and I'd bring her to him the next day. Sadie was very anxious and paced around the house until I went to bed. When I woke up in the middle of the night, Sadie sat on the end of my bed with her nose peering through the blinds. Every time a vehicle came near she would stand up, wag her tail, and run to the door. I finally realized that she was wait-ing for Jim to come home. That morning I immediately took her back to Jim. What a reunion that was. Each of his dogs has been very special. It didn't matter if he couldn't throw a ball or pet them the way other people do. The dogs still loved him unconditionally. You could tell that they sensed how he felt for them just by their actions. They were always very attentive to him. Nikki his current dog was adopted at the age of six and immediately adjusted to him and her new life. Always at his side and aware of what is going on.

Jim and I have unconditional love for each other. Just like any brother and sister, we can fight like the best of them and irritate the hell out of each other but a grudge is never held. Through the years I have seen him grow and become quite independent and sometimes more than I realize. At times, I'm overprotective and see only red and not reason and am quickly told by him that he can make his own decisions and that if he wanted my input he'd ask for it. He immediately puts me in my place but gently by spelling, "I hope you don't get mad at me" or "I hope you understand where I am com-ing from but this is none of your business."

It is hard for me to let go because I want the best for him *all* the time. I find it most difficult to say, "No" when it comes to Jim. Even when I'm totally exhausted, the word "no" just is not been a part of my vocabulary. Why? Because I think I need him probably more than he needs me!

He is the best friend anyone could ask for! I love him so very much!

Brother, John Grimm

It has been hard for me to start this for my brother Jim. I have read a couple of the other writings from other people and immediately felt not up to the task. I have always looked at Jim as just my brother. Maybe a unique brother, but still just my brother.

Our experience as brothers in many ways is very similar to the experiences of other brothers. We shared a bedroom when we were young. We liked to race, but rather than race each other I used to race with him while pushing his stroller or wheel chair. We both usually enjoyed it quite a bit. When everything went well his eyes lit up and his whole face smiled. Sometimes things did not turn out so well. Twice, the front wheel of his chair caught a rock or the edge of the sidewalk and he flipped over forward, landing face first on the ground and me flying over the chair. He ended up with a broken nose after one of the flips. To remember that still makes me cringe. But even after these accidents he still liked to run every once and awhile. I probably did not push him quite as fast.

As far as sharing a bedroom with Jim, it really was not a big deal. He usually slept through the night. The only time I can remember that it was a problem was when he had a broken leg. He got the broken leg during one of our families Sunday evening wrestling sessions. Our dad would sit on the floor holding Jim and then Mary and I would take turns running at Dad and Jim and try to knock them over. It was great fun. We did this just about every Sunday night without any injuries. But one night Mary ran into Dad and Jim and must have fell a little funny. Jim's leg was in the wrong place at the wrong time. Jim ended up with a full cast on his leg. At night he would get terrible cramps in his leg. I think he woke up the whole neighborhood.

As an older brother I still occasionally picked on him to see what kind of a reaction I could get out of him. I always knew when I had ticked him off because his forehead wrinkled up and his eyes burned right through me. If he could talk I am sure every four-letter expletive would have flown out of his mouth. Occasionally someone would spell them out for him. I didn't need them spelled out; I knew exactly what he was thinking.

One of my favorite stories I like to tell about Jim is how we learned how to communicate with him or how he learned to communicate with us. In late 1972 our dad took a sabbatical from work and our family traveled the United Kingdom and Europe. While we were there we started asking Jim to stick out his tongue to answer yes or no. While we were driving in Germany (Jim thinks it was England and Dad thinks it was Norway), Mary or I asked Jim to stick out his tongue ten times, and he stuck it out ten times. Then he did it 50 and then 100 times. The whole family was excited. Then we started having him spell words by going through the alphabet. Jim would stick out his tongue at the letter he wanted to choose. Spelling sentences shortly followed. This opened up a whole new world for all of us. Over the years many different things have been tried to improve Jim's communication and none have been as simple or effective.

During this same time we started playing the card game concentration with Jim. It was amazing the number of pairs he could find without having to do any searching. I thought he had ESP or something. Well Jim does not have ESP, but he does have a good memory. When we played we usually did it on the floor with Jim lying down across from us. Since his head was at floor level he could see each card as it was laid down. He would remember where quite a few of the pair were. It took awhile to figure out how he did it, and he never gave us a clue as to how he did it either. He is a good player even without peeking.

Jim is an amazing person with an amazing drive and spirit. There are also a lot of amazing people that have helped Jim along the way.

The one time I underestimated Jim's abilities was when he got his first electric wheelchair. I think Jim was 18. I grew up with the understanding that Jim could not control his muscles very well (except his tongue of course). So, when I heard he was going to get an electric wheel chair and control it with knee and foot switches I was a little skeptical. I knew he would have some control, but I thought he would be running into things and when he got excited he would wheel around wildly. Well, I was wrong, very wrong. When he was running his wheel chair he was in perfect control. He could maneuver his chair better than I could when I was pushing him. He never cut a turn short! It was also very fun to see Jim experience some mobility and independence. His whole life he had been dependant on other people to get him around and now he was free! I still remember his huge smile and sparkling eyes when he first started. I think everyone has a similar experience when they start driving.

One of the advantages Jim has being handicapped is that he can get great tickets to sporting events and concerts. He was a season ticket holder to the Vikings for a number of years. The seats he had were in the first row, upper deck. They were great seats to watch a football game. Jim has been a loyal Viking's fan for a long as I can remember. I think he would still be a season ticket holder if the Vikings could consistently play well and the tickets were not so expensive. For concerts, the handicap seating is usually pretty good. I have been to many concerts with Jim: Bon Jovi, Aerosmith, Eric Clapton, Bruce Springsteen, Pink Floyd, Metalica and Guns n

Roses are the first to come to mind. Jim has been to many other concerts. Pink Floyd was probably the best concert I have been to with Jim. The concert was at the Metrodome and the seats were on the field. The acoustics were great and the light show was spectacular. We were close enough to see David Gilmore play his guitar. Jim's favorite concert is probably the one where he and Mary went back stage to meet Eric Clapton.

Up until four or five years ago, I thought Jim would live as long as anyone else. Then Jim got pneumonia. He had pneumonia two or thee times within a year. It was a very difficult time for the whole family. We thought Jim's body was starting to deteriorate. That is when I found out that it is not uncommon for people with cerebral palsy to die from pneumonia. Being confined to a wheelchair is not conducive to a healthy respiratory system, and you need to have a healthy one to fight pneumonia. Luckily, it wasn't his body starting to deteriorate that caused the pneumonia; it was the Botox injections he was getting to help his arm spasms. A little bit of the Botox had gone to his throat and caused some of his food to aspirate into his lungs. Needless to say he stopped getting Botox injections.

Jim has had aspiration pneumonia twice since stopping the Botox injections. The last bout of pneumonia he had was the worst. He was in intensive care for a long time. When I saw him heavily sedated, having a tracheostomy, and hooked up to a ventilator, it was the first time I ever felt sorry for him. It was a long recovery for Jim. But being a fighter, he is back to his old self. The hardest part for him was not being able to eat because of the tracheostomy. He did not have any fun during the holidays watching everyone else feed their faces.

That is no longer a problem. Recently, he had a larenjectomy so he can eat again. I wish I had seen the smile on Jim's face when he had his first piece of prime rib.

Growing up with Jim has made me the person I am today. I would not change a single second of the experiences we have shared together. Jim is the only brother I have ever had, wanted or needed. He has had a greater impact on my life than I have had on his, and I thank him for that.

Care Provider, Chelsey Sands

For a man that cannot speak, in the traditional sense of the meaning, James Grimm says so much. His story is an amazing one, and I am so thankful I have had the opportunity to work with him. Jim Grimm will forever hold a very special place in my heart; he is one of the most amazing individuals I have ever met. His life story, with the challenges and obstacles he has faced and overcome, is one I wish everyone could be exposed to in the capacity I have been fortunate enough to experience.

In December of 2005, I began working for a company located in Fridley, Minnesota, called *Life by Design.* This company specializes in bringing care, support, and assisted living to individuals and families. Shortly after, I was fortunate enough to be hired to care for Jim, who has cerebral palsy complicated by scoliosis and other physical handicaps, requiring a staff member to be present twenty-four hours a day. Jim is confined to a wheelchair and is non-verbal. However, he has a unique method of communication. Talking with Jim consists of spelling out the alphabet, one letter at a time. When you reach the letter Jim wants, he moves the corner of his mouth. By combining letters to make words, sentences, and phrases, Jim is able to communicate what his thoughts, needs, and wishes are. At first, this was a tedious process, but after getting to know Jim, one can start using contextual clues to make some guesses as to what Jim might say, even though he does not like people to make too many assumptions. Jim likes to freely express his thoughts. Other staff responsibilities include monitoring and administering medication, upkeep of house and yard, and helping Jim to be as comfortable as possible.

When I first started this job, I felt somewhat apprehensive about the medical involvement and responsibilities associated with Jim's daily needs. Jim had a trachea up until the beginning of the summer that needed to be cleaned out every few hours. He gets his medication via a tube connected to his stomach. He also gets his (liquid) food and water through this tube. After working with Jim for a while, I realized he is like any other human being with feelings, passions, hopes, dreams, and goals. I got comfortable taking care of Jim's medical needs after a short time; his routine includes a detailed record book to make sure the requirements are met.

An expression I have realized the fullness of is, "It's not what's on the outside, but what's on the *inside* that truly matters." Underneath Jim's "handicapped" crippled body is a heart of gold and an ambitious spirit that amazes most who have had the privilege of meeting him. Jim's family, as well as the caretakers and supervising staff that are responsible for Jim's well being, are all *very* supportive and committed to helping Jim live the best life possible. Jim has seen and done more in his forty years than many have done in a lifetime. From listening to thoughts and stories of his friends and family, I know Jim has touched many lives by his example of endurance, sacrifice, patience, and acceptance. Working with Jim has made me better understand the importance of relying on the assistance of others. None of us can make it through this life without the love and support of those around us. I have realized not to take the simple things in life for granted such as being able to breathe on my own or talk with a friend over lunch. I have resolved to consistently thank people and tell those I love how much they mean to me sooner than later. Jim has taught me not to take circumstances, the people in your life, or your health for granted; for we are never guaranteed any of these things will be there tomorrow.

The Bible advises in Matthew 6:34, "therefore, do not worry about tomorrow, for tomorrow will worry about itself. Each day has enough trouble of its own." Many people assert to "live each day to the fullest," but Jim brings a real-life, true example of this philosophy. Through working with Jim, I have realized the meaning of setting priorities and taking time for the truly important things in life. Laundry and other housework can wait if there is something important to discuss or a question that needs to be answered. Not catching every single line of a movie due to discussion about a favorite part or sharing a joke, is okay. Jim has a way of inspiring me to worry less about the insignificant details of life that can easily take up my time and thoughts; and to enjoy the people and blessings more that I so often take for granted.

Isaiah 40:31 confirms that "those who hope in the Lord will renew their strength. They will soar on wings like eagles; they will run and not grow weary, they will walk and not be faint." I had heard this scripture many times before, but not until this winter when I received a significantly important email did I realize more about this verse. It explained where my life was at in the physical-worldly sense as well as in my personal-spiritual realm.

In August 2005, I made the decision to resign from the United States Military Academy, where I had attended for two years, to pursue other educational, personal, and spiritual goals with my life. This was a very challenging transition for me. In addition, my eighty-five-year-old grandmother went to be with the Lord in September. Needless to say, combined with other events, this was a very trying period in my life. However, I believe the Lord's promise that He never gives you more than you can handle. My friend explained in the email how phenomenal a creature eagles are. Because of their body size and weight, eagles tire easily in storms. It is only when they learn to soar, to lock out their wings, can they fly to endless heights and distances in the worst storms and not grow tired. Furthermore, this act enables them to lift and fly with weights up to double their own; in other words, they can "carry" another without getting fatigued.

After going through a rather "turbulent storm" in my life this fall, I truly believe the Lord brought Jim and I together to carry some of one another's burdens and weight. I think we have both grown and learned a lot from each other. It was definitely meant to be; I thank the Lord each and every day for such a wonderful experience and friend to share this "chapter" of life with.

Jim and I sure have shared some great times together and have had many humorous, memorable, and inspiring experiences and conversations with one another. Jim and I have watched the Minnesota Timberwolves play basketball (or should I say that I watch the game, while Jim is usually busy enjoying the "added bonus" of watching the team's cheerleading squad dance on the side line). We got the opportunity to attend the "Evening with Joel [Osteen]" event at the Minneapolis Target Center free of charge for helping hand out programs and pens when people came in the door for the event. I got to go on a family vacation with the Grimm's to Chicago for a long weekend.

We drove Jim's van over, stayed right downtown, and did some fun sightseeing and got some much-needed R and R. Jim and I have watched and discussed numerous movies at theatres and on Jim's big wide-screen T.V. in his home; some of which had deep and thought-provoking story lines, and some light-hearted "chick flicks" that Jim compromisingly agrees to watch every once in a while. Jim loves listening to music and has an extensive CD collection. While listening to a variety of songs one evening, as we often do, we came across the song entitled "Calling All Angels" by the music group Train.

I think it is wonderfully amazing how certain songs can touch your heart and you can relate to them after various experiences you undergo in life. As we listened to the lyrics of this song, Jim and I both agreed that this song portrayed our relationship in a very unique way. Every word makes sense in some way or another to the experiences we have had together. Ever since, we have claimed "Calling All Angels" as "our song" and listen to it frequently. Whenever I hear the song, (and it plays on the radio quite frequently), I immediately think of Jim, and probably always will.

Another day that stands out in my mind was traveling to Hastings school with Jim and his mother to allow Jim to share some of his experiences, struggles, and encouraging achievements with a group of teachers, educators, and other various members of the community. It was so inspiring to observe people's reactions to Jim's story. We have gone out to dinner with friends and family, which is always a good time. Every time we go out into the community I realize some of the challenges and struggles Jim deals with, and I am reminded of my admiration for Jim; he faces life with such perseverance and dignity.

When I tell people about Jim, even after a brief conversation, I can tell that they are touched as well. I find myself bragging about my awesome friend to family members, friends, and many other people that come across my path. Jim and I have taken many walks since the weather started getting better; around local parks and lakes, both with and without his poodle Nikki. We participated in the Humane Society's "Walk for Animals" this spring, which was a great experience. It was a beautiful day to be outside! We also attend *Living Word* church services when we can or when there is a special event going on. While all of these activities are fun and enjoyable, some of my most unforgettable and impacting shifts have been when Jim and I just visit and ponder philosophical questions and opinions, lessons we've learned, and thoughts about the great mysteries and questions of life.

Jim has definitely passed the best-guy-friend-in-the-whole-wide-world test. He has sat and listened to me vent about love, life, relationships, stresses of choosing a college and career, feeling fat, trying new diets (that don't seem to work), and last but not least accompanying me on an emergency trip to the store and rolling down the "embarrassing-avoided-at-all-costs-by-most-men" aisle to purchase feminine products.

Just recently, we had an unforgettable accident happen while I was putting Jim into bed. I failed to get all four straps of Jim's *EZ-lift* machine off the hooks before moving the main machine out of the way. Jim rolled completely over as it pulled him; then actually fell off the bed onto the ground!

I was completely hysterical while Jim was spelling to me that he was fine. He suffered a small cut on his forehead, and had a nice shiner for about a week and a half. We thought about making up a really good bar fight story, but decided against that idea. However, Jim had company come visit that next weekend. One of his best friends in the whole wide world, (who is also mentioned in several places in Jim's book) Dennis, came from Washington, D.C. with his mother from New York and caretaker from Kenya who is going to school in Virginia.

We had a great time talking, eating, and addressing both deep and funny, light-hearted topics of discussion throughout the weekend. It was great to finally meet Dennis. What a great guy with another amazing story! So I got a few "stabs" from the company, as well as from other friends that were visiting for the weekend (you know who you are!) about Jim's black eye. That is okay; I did deserve it! I think I will always be remembered as the staff who dropped Jim and gave him a black eye! I did learn from it though! I definitely realize the glaring importance *not* to become so "comfortable" in your routine that you forget to pay attention and check the details. This is especially true when working with a special friend who has such a fragile body; who has no control over his movement when getting into and out of bed. I felt so bad. I was just so sorry that I made such a stupid, avoidable mistake as that! But Jim was okay. It definitely could have been worse, but I believe we had an angel watching over us that night who kept Jim from getting seriously injured!

Another monumental event that has taken place this summer was Jim's surgery to remove his trachea. He is now able to eat small bits of food and drink liquids of choice, which was a long-awaited and highly anticipated change for

Jim and his family! Jim has a stoma now that needs to be kept clean and taken care of, but no longer has as many physical cares or worries of aspiration. I will never forget the look on Jim's face the day after his surgery; one that spelled relief and a newfound freedom. I can't imagine not being able to eat my favorite foods for a week, much less months and years! It is also nice to see Jim able to drink water. Doctors stress the importance of drinking our recommended amount of water every day. I don't think a lot of people really do this on a regular basis. I take it for granted to be able to enjoy a large glass of water any time I want. Jim has made me more aware of being able to notice and appreciate the little things in life.

In conclusion, I believe in divine appointments; God brings people together in His timing for special purposes. There is no doubt in my mind that God brought Jim and I together during this season of our lives for many reasons; some of which we may not even realize yet. I only hope that people who meet Jim will continue to recognize what an awesome opportunity and privilege it is to get to know such an amazing person, his family, and all those who work together to positively impact his daily life. I also pray that the people whom God places in Jim's life will continue to gain the numerous insights that he has to offer.

Everyone has his or her own story, thoughts, advice, and wisdom to be shared. Working with Jim has given me new perspective on many things. I look forward to the remainder of our time together; Jim and I both know we will really miss each other when I move away and return to college, but I am confident that I have found a life-long friend, and another special second family here in Minnesota. It's not every day one can be fortunate enough to meet someone like James Grimm, as well as his family and all those who work for and with him. I am thankful God has afforded me this opportunity, through working for *Life by Design*. Mine is a heart and *life* that is forever changed as a result of knowing Jim! I wish every person in the world could, sometime during their life, find such a wonderful teacher, mentor, and friend, as I have found in James Grimm.

Friend, Dennis Heaphy

Two things come immediately to mind when I think of Jim: women's breasts and the Vikings football team. Though I appreciate his love of women's breasts, I do not understand his dedication to the Vikings.

Jim and I met almost twenty years ago at the Courage Center, a transitional living facility in Minnesota. The focus of the Center was on the person not the diagnosis. Courage had the feel of a college dormitory and was fantastic. Food fights, late-night conversations, laughter, romance, testing boundaries, and self-discovery were all part of the Courage Center experience. The normality of the experience was poignant and ironically comical.

Now every dormitory has a guy who gets special favors and attention from the women. Jim was that guy at Courage Center. I think he laid his head against the breasts of just about every woman at Courage. Whether it was for eating or "resting," Jim usually managed to have his head nestled against some woman! Envious as I was, I talked to him anyway. And when he wasn't "busy" he managed to find time to talk with me.

Newly disabled and feeling like one of the screwed up toys on Rudolph the Red Nosed Reindeer's Misfit Island I was impressed by the tenacity and surprised by the normality of my fellow residents who had been disabled since birth. It was humbling. I was especially drawn to Jim and his family. The Grimm family is kind of a super magnet that attracts anything within spitting distance. And you should see Jim spit.

The first time I met Jim I thought of him as just another misfit on the island. It was one of those "okay, time to meet another compatriot in my new world." I got far more than I expected. The meeting was actually more of a family affair than a one-on-one meeting. As pretty as she is I cannot remember whether Mary made the introduction or if it was one of her parents. When introduced I received what I would come to learn to be a standard Grimm line, "This is Jim. Jim is just like everyone else, but can't speak. He can communicate using his tongue. Can't you Jim?"

Quicker than a retractable tape measure, out of Jim's mouth came that reptilian tongue that only Gene Simmons from KISS would envy. Thank God it was accompanied by that equally huge smile of his and confirming eyes. That was it. Jim and I have been friends since that day.

It took time and a lot of patience on Jim's part but I finally figured out how to communicate with Jim. I still suck at reading his tongue, but we manage. One of the funniest things I have experienced over the years in talking with Jim is keeping up with his train of thought.

Back at Courage we would be having an intense conversation about politics. I would be concentrating intensely trying to remember all the words he had already communicated when all of a sudden he would switch subjects. It went something like this:

"ABCD. . . ." Sorry Jim can you repeat that last word again I forget what we were talking about. "ABCD. . . ."

Yes the situation is difficult. "ABCD. . . ." It is difficult. "ABCD. . . ." The situation is getting. No that's not what you're saying? "ABCD. . . ." I don't understand "the situation GETL" Jim, what the hell is GETL? I have no idea what you're talking about. "ABCD. . . ." GETLAUR! Shit, get Laurie? Yes? Yes, I'll go get Laurie. I'm sorry I'm so stupid.

He would smile with his tongue hanging out.

As time went on it became, "Shit, get Laurie? you SOB, we're having this intense conversation and in the middle of it you stop because you want Laurie! Maybe I want Laurie, why should you have her! I know I am boring, but give me a break." And he would smile laughingly with his tongue hanging out.

Laurie was Jim's *favorite* attendant at Courage Center. Laurie possessed attributes that we all admired, especially Jim. Without going into detail I will just say that James had more opportunity to take advantage of those attributes than any other resident at Courage. This is no doubt why Jim always interrupted our conversations to request Laurie. It is the only reason I can think of, because I know I am not boring. Now if I could only figure out why he still interrupts to request other people when we talk!

Although we live hundreds of miles apart from each other we have managed to come together to share some wonderful times; His trips to Boston and New York with family in tow; my trips to Minnesota with my mother in tow. We have also shared sad times together including the reelection of President Bush.

Our bond is difficult to describe and probably all but impossible for able-bodied people to appreciate. We share a connection that is rooted in the brokenness of our bodies and a struggle to maintain spirits that are whole. It is a brotherhood born out of struggle despite our differences and yet it is more.

Our mutual struggle is often not our disabilities themselves. We struggle with the insults that come with being disabled: sitting in our chairs staring at a wall for what seems like endless periods of time because nobody notices our positioning. Feeling hunger pains but not being able to eat because we need somebody to "feed" us. Urinating and defecating on ourselves and having to sit in our soiled clothes waiting for someone to clean and dress us. The list could go on.

As I stated above, Jim likes watching the Vikings play football. I prefer reading about the history of the Viking people. Jim grew up traveling all over the world and living in different countries. I was raised in suburban New York. Jim is Lutheran, which I try not to hold against him, and I am a member of the "one true faith." Jim has a sister who would never date me, and I have three brothers who would never date Jim. Jim likes heavy metal and I prefer pop or alternative rock. He is a stick figure and I am a donut. Jim looks like Gene Simmons and I look like Meatloaf. I will let the reader decide who is better looking.

There are other differences as well. Jim was born with cerebral palsy, which resulted in his being unable to communicate verbally, and with spasticity so intense that he needs to use a manual wheelchair that conforms to his body shape. I have a spinal injury resulting in paralysis below the shoulders and using a chin controlled motorized wheelchair.

Unable to express himself verbally without a "tongue" reader, Jim is often isolated in his own thoughts and frustrations. I can speak and can never appreciate the world of silence that Jim lives in so much of the time. Jim would be unnoticed and dismissed if not for his inner strength and thirst for life. This has come with costs. Jim needed to be labeled as "MR" in order to receive some benefits. A person should not have to be mentally retarded to receive support or be labeled as mentally retarded in order to receive medical care and housing.

Despite our differences, you put Jim and me alone in a room together in our manual wheelchairs and we are both helpless in the sense of physical self-care, and hopeless in terms of the prognosis for our mutual conditions. The emotions of strangers vary. Looking at us sitting together evokes pity in many, fear in others, and revulsion in others still. The pity really goes to the on looking strangers who unable to look beyond the physical to see a friendship that has spanned almost twenty years. A friendship rich in humor, strengthened through sadness and forged in love.

We live our lives not according to our own schedules but according to the schedules of others on whom we rely. We wonder and worry, "Will I have somebody to take care of me today?" There are the too many faces of caretakers who come through our doors. People we wished we've never met and hope we will never meet again. There is also the coping with constant goodbyes to people we wished would stay a lifetime and getting accustomed to new people we hope will be compassionate and a friend. There are many times when I need to connect with Jim or his family just to feel whole. We do not need to have a dialogue. Just to hear his gurgling on the other another phone line is enough.

Jim has taught me the value of human life and the terms that go beyond physical understanding. According to the standards of many public health officials, Jim would be considered "a life unworthy of living." He has not achieved any great goals financially or materially. He has made no great contributions to science or held any lofty political office. Without having achieved these worldly goals he has achieved the most important goal of all which is to receive love and to share that love with others.

His confidence and determination are attributes that I do not hold, but through our friendship I am learning their value and seek to integrate them into my life. A dogmatist might be aghast at some of Jim's escapades, but they would've missed the point. Jim has received every moment of life as a gift, many of which he has had to fight for. Like the protagonist in "The Rainmaker," Jim has brought manna to the barren fields that are the lives of so many people. And like every gift from God, Jim's are given on a day to day basis with no promise for what will be tomorrow save the hope that God will always be present in our lives through the many gifts he has given us.

For someone who has never verbalized a word or moved an inch under his own volition, he has made many of the most profound statements ever uttered and moved mountains in ways unseen. I am grateful to have him call me friend. One of the greatest gifts Jim has given me beyond our friendship is a family that has welcomed me as its own. The table of banquet at the Grimm house is never full. At any given moment one can find a stranger brought out of the byways and alleyways of the world invited to dine at a table that any King would enjoy.

Personal Care Attendant, Lisa Rhome

I got to know Jim by working for an agency called Becklund Home Health Care as a personal care attendant. When I started working for Jim, I was simply amazed by the ability of a man who could accomplish anything, but yet had no control of his body because of his cerebral palsy. He was very intelligent, wise and demanding of his personal needs.

As we know, Jim communicates by saying the alphabet and getting to a letter and he would stick out his tongue. This communication method seemed to come easily to me. Jim and I would sit around and talk about anything and everything. When I met Jim, he lived in the Bungalows. His apartment was on a dead-end street. One of my fondest memories from there was when Jim tried running an electric wheelchair with his toe. He went round and round in circles for hours. He bounced off of car bumpers and liked to get stuck in the dirt. Then I would have to go push him out. I laughed so hard because he was so out of control.

He has gone through many devices for communication, such as toe switches, head gear and many more, but has not yet found a quicker method of communication than the ABCs. Jim and I have gained an awesome friendship over the years that will never end. I have known him now for thirteen years. We have many memories that will never be forgotten. I envy Jim because he never gives up. He went from eating 16 oz. T-bone steaks, baked potatoes, veggies, sometimes dessert and a couple of drinks on the side to eating absolutely nothing. His spirits are always uplifting to me.

Jim and I are always on the go whether it's a baseball, football, or basketball game, concert, or just simply people watching at the mall. We like to go, go go. Just being out and about, we always have some kind of story to tell by the time we get home. From someone anonymously buying us dinner, to laughing about the lap dance he got at his favorite place where he is treated as a VIP.

Jim, you are definitely a special person to me and my

family. My girls adore you and have learned a lot from being around you about how handicapped or disabled people are no different from anyone else. We admire your persistence on how you can accomplish anything you want to get done. You are a well-organized man and have the patience of a saint. Jim, you will always have a special place in my heart.

Friend, Bob Neumann

"Jim Grimm is an extraordinary person. Extraordinary because of who he is, what he does and how he affects others.

I met Jim in 1994. I am proud to be able to call him my friend. James is the most patient and ambitious person I know. Jim communicates with facial gestures. As you say the alphabet, Jim makes a positive gesture when you say the letter he wants. Letter after letter, he spells out sentences. If Jim has something on his mind, he will not be silent. This takes an incredible amount of ambition and patience on his part.

Jim has a great sense of humor. He likes to give humorous jabs at his friends and family. Jim will also be the first person to laugh when his friends and family give him a humorous jab.

Jim has a passion for sports that most coaches could not match. I believe the Minnesota Vikings would have won a Superbowl if Jim was on the coaching staff. James was a season ticket holder of the Minnesota Vikings for years. You have to be patient to be a Vikings fan.

Jim is generous. He knows I am a Dallas Cowboys fan. One year, James took me to see the Cowboys play the Vikings. We are both faithful to our teams, so James wanted to make a wager on the game. The loser would buy the winner dinner. That year, Dallas won in the final minutes in classic textbook

Vikings fashion. James was a good sport and bought me dinner. I love to remind him of that game. James is still a Vikings fan, but now he is a Timberwolves season ticket holder.

James is also an ambitious fan of music. James has been to more concerts than anyone I know. One time he even got back stage to meet Eric Clapton. James has a picture of Eric Clapton standing next to him hanging on his wall. I love to see the look of joy in Jim's face in that picture.

Jim has more courage than anyone I know. I work as an R.N. in an ICU. In 2003, I found myself caring for Jim as a patient. Jim was in with pneumonia. He had been removed from the ventilator earlier that day and was now breathing on his own. One of Jim's caretakers was there to assist with communicating with the staff. Jim's face lit up when he saw me walk into the room to be his nurse. It was tough to see my friend so ill. As it got later, I could tell that Jim was starting to struggle with his breathing. I asked him if he wanted to be put back on the ventilator. Jim gave me the positive facial gesture. Shortly after that, he lost his ability to make facial expressions because of exhaustion. I was not sure he could even hear me, but I informed him of everything that was happening. I talked him through the procedure and reassured him that his sister was on her way to the hospital. His sister arrived just prior to Jim being put back on the ventilator. She was able to let Jim know that she was there for him. I later learned that Jim was aware of all I had said.

Jim's family set up a rotating schedule and remained at the hospital during the remainder of his recovery. They assisted Jim with communicating with the staff. After much consideration, Jim made the decision to have a tracheotomy to assist with his breathing. Jim recovered after several weeks in the hospital. Jim does not like having a tracheotomy, but he has learned to adapt to it. Jim has an incredible ability to adapt to change.

Jim used to love eating with friends and family. A couple years ago, Jim lost his ability to swallow food safely without choking. He now received nutrition via a tube in his stomach. I know this was another difficult change for Jim to accept. Like a true champion, he has adapted once again. Jim recently took my family out to dinner even though he is no longer able to eat himself.

Jim is extraordinary because of his courage and patience. His ability to adapt to adversity truly inspires me. He is a giver, even when so much has been taken from him. Jim ambition to enjoy life, for what life is, is an example to the rest of us. Jim is extraordinary because he makes me want to be a better person. When a person is able to influence another in such a way, he is Extraordinary!

Personal Caretaker, Amber Boen

Jim is an inspiration to me. I came to work with him only a few months ago. Although it has been only a few months, it feels like a lifetime. Jim and I agree that God meant for us to meet. Jim, like me, has a very outgoing personality; we are both patient and we both love to joke around. Not to mention, we love the same music. Jim and I have spent many nights talking and laughing until two in the morning, and we end our nights cranking up the music until the next shift comes on. Jim is the kind of friend that when I don't see for a few days, I kind of miss. He is the person that listens to me no matter what and never hesitates to give me his input. He is always so concerned about the things I do, and is very respectful of my decisions. Jim has shown me there is so much to be grateful for in life. When I was growing up, I had always known what I wanted to do with my life, but after a few twists and turns I was confused again. Working with Jim has truly put me on the right track of following my dreams. Jim has let me know that my personality and my kindness will allow me to soar to new heights. I don't know what I would do if I didn't know this man.

He is the person that lights up a room with his smile, his laugh and his unique personality. No matter how bad some days are, he always puts a smile on his face and those around him. As far as I know, we do the same for him. There is no such thing as a negative attitude when Jim is around. He goes out of his way to keep the most positive attitude in every situation that we have encountered. My life motto is to laugh and smile because that is the only way to make it through the day. I think Jim is a perfect example of my motto.

Our relationship is truly a great friendship. We both would agree. We talk about life, friends, family relationships; and although Jim is the kindest, sweetest man ever, he does have his "bad" side. I think if I could pick a song for Jim, it would be "Bad To The Bone." He is exactly that. He loves women, and I hope some day he finds a girlfriend that makes him as happy as he makes the rest of his staff. Jim has tried his "bad" side from time to time (with me), but I set him straight real quick and because of that, we will always be friends. Jim, you know exactly what I am talking about.

I guess it is hard to put in words the reality of our friendship. A lot harder than I ever imagined. But I want you to know Jim that no matter what happens in life, I am proud to have ever known you. Whether I move away, or I finish school and move on to my career, whether you get sick of me and find a new staff, or whatever else this life has in store for us, you will always have a huge part of my heart. The memories that I have of you in only a few short months, I will cherish forever. You have honestly made me the person that I am and the person I am yet to become. You have put a smile on my face in the hardest of times, and you taught me that even AC/DC isn't that bad! You are the bravest, smartest, kindest and most patient man I have ever met. You are a huge admiration to me and many other people. I love our friendship so much and I would never change a thing. I promised you before and I promise you now, I will never lose touch with you. No matter what happens. I thank God for giving me this opportunity to be a part of your life. I thank you for allowing me to be a part of it.

Aunt, Carol Crosby

James Wilson has always had a special place in our hearts and always will. We have many special and interesting things we have shared over the years. We were in the road construction business and always a lot of activity at our place. I don't believe I ever missed calling Jim on his birthday, even when he was in England. When he was little we would try to get him to pronounce words and one of those words was onion. Why onion I can't remember, but when we called him in England on his birthday he said "onion." I always thought that was special. One of the most dangerous things was to go with Uncle Keith on the bulldozer to push out trees. They accomplished the job with a smile on their faces. Then we raised chickens for a number of years and every October at MEA time we would butcher chickens. Jim, Mary, John, and Mom and Dad would spend the weekend. Not the most pleasant job but we always had fun and many laughs. Mary like to check out the innards and do some dissecting, and the feet really interested James. Well, cousin Brenda took some chicken feet and fish line and tied the line on the tendons or muscle, so when you pulled on the fish line the claws would move. James could not wait to show his friends. That was fine, but they forgot about the feet in his backpack and need-less to say James was rather smelly till they remembered the chicken feet. Having a number of grandchildren stopping by when the Grimms were visiting sometimes was a challenge, and the younger ones often questioned why is this feller in this chair and why doesn't he talk.

Jim took it very well, but once one of them decided he is just a big baby and he needed toys. His chair got filled with rattles and soft little toys. One thought he or she had done a good job, and dear James just smiled and chuckled.

It took a few years before we understood why it was okay to stay home with his big cousins, Galen and Jeff. We found out later they took James to the barn, up the ladder to the hay mow, and put him on their swing. They had made of a gunny sack filled with straw, which hung from the roof called a sling rope. Galen and Jeff took turns with Jim riding a straddle of this bag swing and go from one end of the barn to the other. If I'd realized what was going on, my sons would be getting a talking too. When James eyes were really sparkly, we knew something was up or some one had done something rather interesting. James' eyes say it all. Those big cousins were rather daring and James enjoyed every minute. Right James! From four-wheeling in the ditches, riding in the gravel truck, and pay loaders. Around quitting time each night, Jim (with his Crosby Construction cap on) would sit out on our deck and watch the trucks roll in.

Sometimes we had some hectic moments when you stayed

with us and Mom and Dad were on a trip. He had to put up with me for a few days and we both were so happy to have Brenda here to help in troubling times. Which really were not that bad, except for me being slow at spelling which I am sure was frustrating for him but we made it. I recall a morning of frustration. Somehow I hit the plate of pancake, peanut butter, syrup and we were covered in the mess. Brenda laughed. Also I made him breakfast and thought all was ok, but he insisted he needed something and spelled S- R- P. For the life of me I could not figure it out. Brenda came to the rescue. "More syrup," says Brenda and both of us burst into laughter!

I could go on and on. Some stories are a bit too colorful to write about in this book. Our friends have many memories too, when he was on the computer he told my friend Ruby what he thought of her, and asked our highway patrolmen friend some interesting questions. These are just a few tidbits and memories from the farm.

Next-door Neighbors, Gordy and Michael Dodge

It is Friday, February 3, 2006, and Jimmy's editor has insisted that all contributions to Jimmy's book have to be in by this coming Monday. Besides, Jimmy's Super bowl party is this Sunday, so we'd better pull our thoughts and memories together. It isn't that we don't want to write something about Jimmy, much to the contrary. We are pleased and honored that he has asked us to contribute something, but our relationship with Jimmy has been for so very many years and has so many facets it is difficult to pull out what might be the most important to express.

To benefit the reader's perspective a short history is in

order. With our six children we moved to Center City, next door to the Grimms in June of 1970. Over the past thirty-five years our children played together and grown up together. We have been close friends, and good neighbors to each other. We have worked for many of the same social, political, and community causes with each other, several of which were key to Jimmy's educational, social and health rights and opportunities. Although Jimmy has been out on his own now for several years; like all of our grown children are to Gordy and Esther, and like Johnny and Mary, Gordy and Esther's other two children, are to us, we easily continue to maintain a deep interest in, enjoyment of, and admiration and fondness for Jimmy. The key concept of importance in the previous sentence is "like all of our other grown children," because in spite of all the physical limitations Jimmy has had to and still has to deal with he was so enjoyably a normal and healthy child and teen-ager growing up, and as an adult, has the qualities and character we would wish for everyone.

Most of the credit for Jimmy being the fine man he is of course must be given to Jimmy himself, and his courage, self-confidence, intelligence, care for others, and unmatched sense of humor. However, we have over these many years also admired Gordy and Esther's ability as parents to care for and advocate for Jimmy while still letting him live a normal life, knowing the value of his venturing off with friends even when he was quite young and "helpless" (ha); and neither overprotecting him nor spoiling him. Our children have great memories of fun times together with Jimmy, with no adults interfering, some of which stories we are sure they still prefer not telling us.

There are many trite words, phrases, and lessons learned that we are reluctant to express here, just because they may sound trite. However, they are so true and important that they require mentioning. We have learned more from Jimmy and he has done more for us than we for him, and this applies not only to the two of us but also to our children, our town of Center City, our school system, and our county. When we had the opportunity of caring for Jimmy even when he was quite young (my wife, admittedly, doing much more of the caring for than I) so that his parents could occasionally have a few hours or a few days to themselves, the experience reassured us that good parenting approaches and savvy common sense are sufficient for effective care of most handicapped children. Parents need to be competent and dedicated but it is the smallest percentage of handicapped children who cannot be raised in a normal home and family setting, to the betterment of all.

As a psychologist, I have always held to the belief that communities rather than large governmental institutions are in the best position to assist individuals and families with their overall development and fulfillment. To that end, when Jimmy was quite young, I served on the local school board and a couple of other local non-profit initiatives. Jimmy's needs and rights provided the impetus more than any other individual for significant establishment and improvement of local educational and human services for handicapped children. Jimmy, his family and friends continue to courageously fight for what he and others deserve.

Our local communities and schools not only improved services in response to Jimmy's presence and efforts, but we all learned from Jimmy. I recall when the local high school drama director asked me how he could have the student actors portray mental illness since the play he was doing was set in a state hospital for the mentally ill. Prior to talking with me he had the actors incorporating limb and facial spastic-ity into their body movements. When he and the students were provided examples of Jimmy and other persons with Cerebral Palsy in the community who were of sound intel-ligence and emotional health, this erroneous stereotype was dispelled. What Jimmy brought to his classmates, educa-tional staff, and the community at large, was a much better understanding of, acceptance of, enjoyment of, and respect and appreciation for those among us who at first glance may seem different.

We are thankful for Jimmy growing up as our neighbor, and the friendship we have had with him, his mom and dad, and his bother John and sister Mary. Even more impor-tant, though, are the influences and friendships he has had and still has with our own children. The value of the good times they have had together as well as the times they were there for each other when things weren't so good cannot be quantified. Jimmy kept all of this friendship well grounded with his enthusiasm, inquisitiveness, and loyalty; but most importantly, with his great sense of humor. We especially thank you Jimmy for having been such a good friend with our children. Although you, they, and we no longer live next door to each other we are all still so fortunate for you having been and continuing to be so much a part of our lives. Don't worry. We are sounding a little sappy right now, but writ-ing about you also brings back several very fun and funny memories, with you in the star role.

Next-door Neighbor, Cecelia Dodge

Our family moved to Center City in 1970, the summer be-fore I entered second grade. The Grimms were our next-door neighbors. John and I are the same age. Our two families were back and forth, up and down the hill all the time. My mom and Esther would drink tea and smoke cigarettes and sit at Esther's kitchen table every day. We were very close.

I remember being friends with Jim right away. I would often go play with him after school and on weekends. We had some fun games Jim liked to play. We would play for hours. Jim liked to play office. We had lots of papers stacked on the dining room table, and we would pretend we worked in an office. I don't know exactly what we did but it kept us in a pretend-world that we really got into! We also liked to dance. I remember there was a record player in the room that used to be a three seasonal porch. We played 45s, "Lemon Tree" and "Hey, Hey, We're the Monkees." We would spin and laugh and get all sweaty! We also played "Sandwich." Jim had some giant pillows and Esther would help me transfer Jim out of his chair and stretch him out on a pillow. I put another one on top and squished him between them. This was really fun and good for him. We did this to give him a good stretch so he wouldn't get contractions.

Sometimes I would help feed Jim. I know that his favorite mixed pancakes with peanut butter and milk. They were of a good consistency that would allow Jim to swallow more easily. Eating was really hard for Jim, and it took a long time. Esther always had food around that I liked too. Sometimes there were frozen Snicker bars in the freezer. I believe that I probably wore my braces a few months longer due to one of those frozen Snicker bars.

Center City was such a perfect place to grow up. We liked to walk around the neighborhood, too. We usually walked slowly and went downtown or up to the church. Jim's brother, John, liked to push Jim fast. Jim would laugh and laugh. I remember John tipping Jim's chair over going really fast around the corner of their sidewalk, and Jim went flying out. He thought it was really funny.

I also went with Esther to take Jim to Gillette for medical and dental care. I remember that was the only time I really thought much about Jim's disability and how much harder his life was than mine. I also thought about the fact that even though he was so smart, so much fun, and such a good friend, that he wasn't going to be able to live a normal life. He wasn't going to get married nor have kids. I looked around at all the other kids with disabilities and their families and thought about how their lives were affected. I often thought about what it must be like for Esther and Gordy to raise a child with such significant difficulties. Carrying Jim, toileting, dressing and feeding him—these things were all so difficult. And I thought about John and Mary having this brother, who needed such different things, like having the house remodeled and all kinds of medical care and adaptive equipment. Everyone loves Jim so much *and* their lives are all so different because of him.

It was easy to understand him in those days, and I had confidence that technology was going to help him be able to communicate with more people. That hasn't come to pass, unfortunately. He would light up his face and stick out his tongue and make positive vocalizations when he agreed. He would scowl and make a sad sound if he disagreed. I've been disappointed that there haven't been any new ways for Jim to communicate. The hardest part for me about Jim's disability is that such a fun-loving and smart person is trapped in a body that doesn't work and he can't communicate when he wants to. I'm sure this is the hardest part for Jim, too!

I think it was during some of these trips to Gillette that I started thinking about working with people with disabilities. Jim did inspire me, first to go into occupational therapy, then into special education. I also volunteered at Gillette helping to build custom seating and lap trays. This was largely due to the time I spent positioning him and hanging out at Gillette. Jim inspires anyone who knows him! He has the best sense of humor and he doesn't get down easily.

I remember doing a project when I was in OT school where I had to write a paper on adaptive equipment. Jim had a cool winter jacket that was split down the middle into two pieces. You could put it on him one side, then the other, and Velcro it together in the front and in the back. This was a stroke of genius because his spasticity and contractions made it very hard to get shirts and jackets on. I think it made so much sense to me that kids with disabilities need to be in school and need to have every opportunity for a normal experience.

I missed the Grimms and especially Jim when they were in England. I do remember wondering how school was going for him over there and if he was making any friends. I also thought that it was pretty cool that probably not too many families with a child with severe cerebral palsy would just pack up and move to Europe for a year or two. So, I was happy they were all having that experience.

Since I grew up and moved away I have not been in touch with Jim as much as I would like to be. I remember the first time, as an adult, that I began to understand that Jim would not live to be an old man. I hadn't really understood how difficult his breathing could get, and how much harder it has gotten for him to eat real food. For some reason I had always thought that things would get easier. But that doesn't make sense medically and I was probably in denial about how awful this disease is and how it will take Jim from us too soon.

I believe Jim was put on this earth to teach us about life and humanity. Jim is amazing and his family is amazing too! There are so many people whose lives have been touched by Jim. So many teachers and students have benefited by having Jim in school. Anyone who knows Jim knows how to look past a wheel chair and a twisted body to see a real person and understand at least a little bit about how different life is for those with disabilities, yet how much the same.

Next-door Neighbor, Nathaniel (Beep) Dodge

Hello James! Memory is a finicky thing for sure and mine can play tricks on me, but when I heard you were writing a book I thought I would throw a few things in the mix and see if it sparked anything for you. A particular incident comes to mind, or maybe it was a series of incidents rolled into one, because I remember it a few different ways.

The crew would come down to your house to see if you wanted to go out. We would walk the neighborhood usually up to the church. The "crew" would consist of Jay, Kyle, sometimes Danny Nelson, maybe one of the Flicke boys, and myself. What we did on these walks varied, and I cannot quite remember specifics, but thinking of the ages 11–15 makes me think we hoped we would run into the girls of the neighborhood, like the Mackrille sisters (Bonnie) and the other one, maybe Katie Rieke, or the exotic Granstrand sisters.

James you were often game for whatever we were up to which comes to the main part of my long-winded memory. We would be getting you home for dinner in the afternoon, and when we arrived at the top of the hill above your house we would ask you if you wanted us to let you roll down to your driveway. Well, we all would laugh and start walking down the street. Whoever was walking you would let go of you chair handles, and it was steep so you would get ahead a few feet and we would catch up to you, slow you down before you careened of into the ditch or zipped out into traffic along the road going by the lake. We all found this very amusing, and I can hear us all laughing uncontrollably. Your laugh is distinctive with a bit of a honk; Danny Nelsons was quiet and hard at the same time.

Anyway I swear there was one time we were doing this, and we could not catch up to you. We would get cocky and let you roll too far. You were gaining speed and ripping towards the county road. Shit I was scared! I think Kyle and Jay were there too. When you passed your driveway, your chair careened to the left and you rolled into your yard and tipped over. We were right behind you and almost caught you, but missed. You landed in the grass. You had been strapped in pretty well and we picked you up in the chair and all. You were unscathed! Not even a scratch! Am I remembering this right? You said you were not angry with us and you brushed apologies aside. As we walked into your house I am sure I was worried that your mother may have seen this, but I don't think she did.

What do you think? Did it all happen this way? I was the youngest you know. Jay, Kyle, and you were older. I hope you get this in your book, and it is helpful. We had a great childhood. I would do those days over again.

Neighbor, Jay Nelson

Some search before finding a lifelong friend. I found one in Jim without effort. We were only two or three when our moms began visiting as neighbors. Jim and I played like most boys with trucks and Legos. Jim watched while I drove his trucks and built his houses. When I wanted to go somewhere I'd grab Jim by the arms and drag him to the next room with me. My mom was horrified the first time she saw it. Esther reassured her that Jim was fine and it was perfectly acceptable between two kids in our situation. I recall many adventurous days playing cops. Unlike some boys with one as the cop and one as the robber, we were always the good guys trying to catch the FBI top ten fugitives together. We spent hours playing and talking when I learned how to communicate with Jim. I often would go over to Jim's house after school on Friday and wouldn't return home until Sunday for dinner.

As we got older, Jim and my interest changed to Rock-n-Roll. Our favorite band was hands down KISS. Complete with make-up and air guitar, I was Paul Stanley and you can guess which member of the band Jim was with that tongue of his. We even caught a KISS concert and the tongue master himself, Gene Simmons. As teenagers through the last couple of years, Jim and I would venture to the Dome to take in a Twins or Vikings game. Using binoculars I would line up a closer view for Jim of the cheerleaders that is.

I think our friendship was hard to maintain at the same level when I was in high school. My interest took me in a different direction with fewer things I know how to include him in on. While the frequency of our time hanging out changed, he was still what you could call a real friend. When others would disappoint me, Jim was always there. While his circumstance made him an obvious listener, he was really good at it. He often helped me to see that some people were not worth investing in and their words not worth worrying about.

When I got married I knew Jim needed to be there. Not as a guest but as part of our wedding party. He was wheeled in first-class, tux and all, and shared in this big day like all my others before.

They say friendships are a two way street. I'm sure Jim would tell you that I've been important to him as well. I gave him arms and legs, and Jim gave me a reason to see differently. I hope I see individuals with traditional disabilities with something different to offer instead of nothing. I wonder if I could be as strong as Jim if I faced the challenges that he has. I have great respect for Jim and his family. They accept and handle everything with amazing faith. Not many people can say they have a friend that has extended from childhood to the present. I know I can depend on this one for life.

Friend, Beth Hawkins

I met Jim Grimm many years ago when he and his family were considering how to purchase his own home and individualized care team. A few years passed before we crossed paths again and this time Jim was determined to move out of a care facility into a home of his own. Jim, his family, and I spent hours dreaming and planning and ultimately found the perfect home for Jim and his friend Cory. Given Jim's physical limitations and significant support needs there were many hurdles to overcome but Jim was not to be denied. The house was remodeled to accommodate Jim and Cory and a "self-directed" support program was created and in May of 2000. They moved into their home and their "regular life."

Over the years that I have known Jim, he has experienced many changes; some were typical, such as when Cory moved out and other housemates moved in; some were life changing, like when he had to get the trachea tube. Jim has had to overcome many obstacles but from my perspective, that is not how I think of Jim. I think of him as a wise and kind person, determined to live his life as a regular guy. Whether it is rocking to his music, going to football games, concerts, nightclubs, or vacationing, he just wants to have a good time, be with people he cares for and make a difference in this world. I am glad to know Jim. He has much to say and offer to others. I am certain that whatever lies ahead Jim will make sure that he remains in charge of his life.

Friend, Ildi Sundheim

Jim, you and your family arrived in my life when I badly needed a reminder how other families live and function, after having been in a community of mainly young adults for approximately seven years at Hothorpe Hall in the middle of England. But did the Grimms bring a sense of "normalcy" for when I return to the U.S.A.? No! But you brought acceptance, enjoyment, lifelong friendship, and interest in those around you. This goes for you especially Jim, as an individual member of your family.

I remember your patience with my attempts at communicating (never mastered it), and helping to hold you in the water at Sunrise and in Sand Lake. You were also patient with my attempts of getting enough nourishment into you when you stayed with us in Lindstrom. Do you remember that?

All this was when you were much younger of course, and I wish we could have stayed in your area. Who knows I might have even learned the ABCs.

My hope is for many more times sitting around a table anywhere with you, Esther, Gordy, Mary, and as many more family members and friends as possible, and seeing your eyes shine with total awareness and participation, getting a good taste of things that matter in this world, according to Jim Grimm.

Friend, Marlyn Sundheim

Jim Grimm, the fisherman. Our paths have crossed many times around the world, including Center City, Lindstrom, and New London, Minnesota, as well as London, England and in the Midlands around Theddingworth Nr. Rugby, at an old manor house called Hothorpe Hall, where you lived with your family for almost one year. That's where our families got to know each other and enjoy being together.

But the story I'd like to share is when your father Gordy and I took you fishing on Sand Lake, about 25 miles north of Deer River, Minnesota. We would start out from Aqua Haven Resort where we stayed in rustic cabins many times. After a big breakfast of pancakes and peanut butter, we were ready to go out and catch the biggest northern pike of the week.

When you were younger, your father would hold you in his lap, making sure you were in contact with the rod and line. As you grew longer and heavier, you were set up in a boat seat, always making sure that some part of your body was in contact with the fishing line.

We were so confident when you were along fishing with us. All you had to do was to play the line a little bit with the Jim Grimm special touch, and another big fish was fooled. It was as though you could talk those fish into the boat. We usually used a Johnson Silver Minnow with pork rind attached and trolled from Aqua Haven over to the Empty Bar Resort nearby. We went back and forth a few times, and then it was time to go back to shore where everyone seemed to have gathered, waiting and expecting a big catch. As you know, Jim Grimm, you never disappointed the crowd or me. Thanks for the worldwide memories.

Friend, Kirsten Topel

I have Jim Grimm to thank for my addiction to peanut butter. I'm quite sure I didn't even know about peanut butter until I met Jim. I took peanut butter on pancakes to the next level by adding bacon and bananas. I still enjoy this combo even to this day (minus the bacon now.). My memory is horrible. At age forty-two, I can't imagine how bad it will be later on. I do however remember the Grimm's coming to Hothorpe Hall, being tormented by John, having another playmate "sister" in Mary, and being intrigued by the little boy in the wheelchair with the beautiful big brown eyes. I remember thinking how neat it was that we could communicate with you in such a different manner than anyone else and how I thought that made your really special. I am impressed with what an influence you have had on so many lives, and though I know life has not been easy for you I admire all you have strived to do. What an inspiration to us all!

Friend, Andrea Brew

Here are my favorite memories of Jim. I'm afraid I don't have the mind of a steel trap, so details often elude me; but I have a good memory for feelings and images, which are vivid when I recall our "detective days."

I remember fondly the days we spent playing detectives in the Grimm's cozy den. We never tired of all the paperwork and planning that detective work seemingly involves. As our captain, Jim was highly effective without being tyrannical. He kept us all in line and made sure things were done properly. After taking care of such details as choosing our names (was I Sergeant Scarlet or Lieutenant Green?), we would proceed to the important business of filling out and stamping multitudes of forms. I think I was a natural little bureaucrat, happily immersed in all of the red tape. Despite the seriousness of our business, we had a lot of laughs. I'll never forget the sound of Jim's laughter and the sparkly mirth in his eyes. Jim's eyes communicate volumes and display all the intelligence, humor, and compassion that a true captain needs. We never had cause for complaint or threatened to go on strike. I may no longer be so fond of paperwork or filling out forms, but I will always recall those long hours of detective work with Jim as being pure and simple—if somewhat bureaucratic—fun.

Former School Teacher, Jim Kelley

I remember when I first heard Jim would be arriving as a student in his first year in the public school. He was assigned to Mrs. Mitchell's first grade classroom, and I was to be his Speech and Language Pathologist. Jim had multiple needs and being totally dependent on someone else for all physical activities, I recall having a variety of feelings about serving a student with such intensive needs. I felt very inexperienced and somewhat overwhelmed by the idea for how best I might meet his needs as a speech clinician.

I remember the first meeting with Jim and his family. I was very anxious. The family was also somewhat nervous about starting Jim in public school. It was amazing how the process developed. Jim was the first student with intensive needs that was to be mainstreamed in the public school. Almost immediately an interactive functioning team began interacting and began to make it work. The deal was a lock the day we met Jim! Jim was a normal thinking first grade boy! He was locked in a body that he had no control over, and we needed to help him feel like a regular kid!

The memories of our experiences could fill another book! I would like to say that Jim and I have become very close friends. He and his family have befriended me throughout our years together. Jim and I have experienced much together, and I have confided in him and he in me. We have followed our favorite teams together and tried to support each other and lend an ear to each other.

Personal Care Attendant and Friend, Amy Teed

When I first met Jim my impression of him was, "he is extraordinary." Jim is a special child of God. He has an important purpose here on earth, to teach us tolerance, patience, kindness and love. Jim is courageous. Jim is a Deep Thinker and a romantic Heart. Jim would make an excellent leader. He has great ideas for our society and the changes that our government needs. How I wish Jim had a voice to rise up the people and start a revolution!

The greatest gift I have received from Jim is to be brave. God's promise, "Those that are last here on Earth will be first in Heaven." I believe that promise is for Jim. I also believe when Jim meets his creator Our Lord will say to him, "Well done, my good and faithful son!"

Assistive Technology Engineer, Marty Stone

First let me tell you how and why I met Jim, then a little about our journey, then few reasons why you need to read his story.

It may have started when I began to like the word *we* more than *I*. Or when I realized running from pain brings more. Let me start here. One of my groups of friends in high school had a great past time. We would jump in the car and drive to Cambridge State Hospital and volunteer with the various departments. In the late 70's it was a busy bustling campus for mentally retarded children and adults. I think it was at Cambridge where I learned to cry unselfishly. It was there I saw babies in cribs that had bars all around and on top; it was there I saw miracles meant only for me. It was there that I was the lady asking the Lord for scraps from his table for her children. I enjoyed it so much that I would often go there on my own when no one was available. It was an especially good year when my family went with me over Christmas to the hospital. Do you see where this is going?

Knowing that I had this unusual past time, Dr. Mike and Mary Clifford (a friend of the family) thought I would really like getting involved with Camp Courage in Annandale, Minnesota where they volunteered time during the summer. So, I took their advice and became a camp counselor for a couple summers while finishing up with college courses in industrial technology. Bob Nelson was my technical inspiration, and professor Mark Larchez was my mentor, as I focused on electronics, physics, and math.

Do you see where this is going now?

The spring of 1983, I landed my first real paying job at a telecommunications company (NorTel Now). Now I was being paid to learn and had time to do other things I liked. So, I walked into Courage Center to see if the Rehabilitation Engineering Group could use any volunteer help. "I have someone that I could use some help with," said Ray Fulford, Courage Center's only rehabilitation engineer back in 1983.

I remember him looking over his shoulder and catching the eye of his assistant (Denny Meyer) who looked at him and meaningfully nodded. He mentioned a few things they had tried.

Now you see where I'm going?

I was on my way to meet Jim at his home in Center City, Minnesota. Who I met first was Esther, one of the absolutely warmest mom's you'd every meet. She looked you straight in the eyes, not your shoes, and with a warm smile and twinkle in her eye you were welcomed! You just wanted to leave so you could come in again!

Then I met Jim, He had the same smile and twinkle. I had just been doubly blessed. Through the course of the afternoon I met his neighbors, friends, and the cat. It was easy to see Jim was well loved and had a great attitude. Cerebral palsy seemed to be the only rain cloud in his otherwise sunny life.

As cerebral palsy goes, Jim has a very severe form. It's effects leave him unable to walk, talk, feed himself, scratch, blow his nose, choose what to look at, who to hug, reposition himself, call for help, climb a mountain, scuba dive, play tennis, pull his sister's hair, wrestle his brother, and at times even to breath. If you want to understand what it is like, duck tape your mouth shut, and then duck tape your arms and legs backwards to a crazy ape. Do this for your whole life, and you will just about have it. If you don't fight the ape, you wouldn't last long. But, if you do, your character will grow and you will be lean, focused, and as you get older very tired. Jim has chosen to fight the ape.

So, in 1983 I chose to join Jim's growing team. Although no one on the team could fight the ape for Jim, the hope is and was to make it more bearable. If you have a hammer you solve problems with hammers; if you have an engineering/

physics background you use those. Here are a few things we tried over the years.

In 1983, through Courage Center, we used a full head band with a hard plastic chin strap that had a switch connected to it. Jim would press the switch with his tongue to access his Apple Computer. Of course in '83, a single switch game was the best you could do. At this time Marty Carlson at Gillette Children's Hospital was also on Jim's team and was attempting to give him wheelchair control with a combination of customized seating system and hard plastic knee cuffs. The cuffs were tethered to a couple pressure switches. If you could use enough force to activate the switches you would be able to move the electric wheel chair. In the 80's anything electric was not very reliable. Wheelchairs topped the list.

In about 1984, Jim came to Camp Courage North in Annandale where Denny Meyer from Courage Center and I started teaching a computer camp for folks with disabilities. This is when I learned Jim's word for a black fly is biting, no eating my ear.

As I was feeding him, he used his eyes to tell me something was wrong. As I was spelling with him to get out what it was, the fly would bite him. So, between Jim, the ape, and the fly, the message wasn't getting across. In the mean time the fly is having his lunch, the ape is doing a jig, Jim is in agony, and I am rattling off letters like an auctioneer and couldn't feel more helpless and incompetent. We were down near the lake, away from the other campers. So I couldn't run for help and leave him. By the time I finally figured out what it was, we were both sweating and relieved. I am sweating now thinking about it.

In January 1994, Jim started working on a 286 computer system that utilizes a custom Morse Code program based on

EZmorse for keyboard emulation, along with an abbreviation expansion program (PRD+). Due to many factors including changing living situations, summers, and mainly fatigue due to work involved in accessing switches, it had little use. Much of the work and research of Jim's switches were done through Gillette Children's Hospital and volunteer time. Jim his family and attendants made it even possible to test various technologies.

By February 1994, Jim's physical ability had been changing. The third digit on Jim's left foot showed relatively fast twitch ability. From the top of Jim's head (tongue included) to his toes, this was the most promising movement for switch activation to date. Mechanical toe switches were fabricated and tested. New software, with the above changes, was loaded. Jim found that switches with a wider activation area would be easier. He also suggested some software modifications. Kellie Steinmetz from Employment Innovations (part of Rise Inc.) then found Jim a job using the above toe switches.

Jim has been tethered to a wheel chair and a switch placed in space for him to hit with his toe. Since Jim needed to be restrained, pressure problems, fatigue, and accessibility to the switch were all variables to its lack of effectiveness. As stated above, these were replaced with foot mountable devices. The foot mountable devices worked fine. However, it was found that the rigid case holding the switches would produce sores over time. They also would drift out of reach over time. The third major disadvantage is having a cable running from his foot to the thing he is controlling.

On September 6, 1995, Jim was seen for an electric wheel chair repair. The problem ended up being minor. A force switch adjustment fixed the problem of the chair spinning in circles. At this same time, Jim gave me feedback on the effectiveness of a new "fuzzy logic toe switch." He hasn't had much time to work with it due to staffing changes. However, he was planning on moving home. He hoped to have a better chance to put the switch to the test.

In January of the next year, after many software, hardware, and mounting iterations, it was reported that Jim, with the help of Lisa Gall (his personal care attendant) had been using the prototype ten hours a week. This prototype became insensitive to variations in placement, was able to determine when a good switch hit has been made through a fuzzy logic scheme that watches toe position. With this switch, Jim could have the capability to change switch characteristics to use for work, Environmental Control Units (ECUs), communication, or recreation.

To this point, all programming, research, and development has been on a volunteer basis. The results of the last three years of research and prototypes around the fuzzy switch design have yielded a device that will bring Jim much independence. At present this prototype demonstrates his ability to access five selections via toe movement.

From 1997 to today, I've worked with Jim. In late November 2006, I met with Jim and his staff. Because his chin movement was now unreliable, I tested a voice recognition system with Jim. The hope is to identify the various sounds he is able to make for control. During this meeting Jim was successful in generating a few sounds. Two sounds where able to be used for control. The next step is to set Jim up with a system that will allow him to practice making these sounds and determine both accuracy/consistency on a daily basis. Sound files were taken of the repeatable sounds. These will be used for his test system. In March of this year, 2007, a sound recognition system is almost ready for Jim to begin testing.

Read Jim's story to be surprised, enlightened, and encouraged by how much you can endure when you love and are loved. No matter if your crazy ape is cerebral palsy, a bad attitude, cancer, depression, hopelessness, self-pity, pride, or all of these, you will find some rest in getting to know Jim through his story. Read it to gain empathy and understanding. To help another with their trials often takes time to understand what they are dealing with. Or, at least, it may allow us to be slow to judge another. I'll end here with a favorite quote from 2 Corinthians 4:16:

Therefore we do not lose heart, but though our outer man
is decaying, yet our inner man is being renewed day by day.
For momentary light affliction is producing for us
an eternal weight of glory far beyond all comparison.

What is Cerebral Palsy?

THE TERM CEREBRAL refers to the brain's two halves or hemispheres, and palsy describes any disorder that impairs control of body movement. Thus, these disorders are not caused by problems in the muscles or nerves. Instead, faulty development or damage to motor areas in the brain disrupts the brain's ability to adequately control movement and posture.

Symptoms of cerebral palsy lie along a spectrum of varying severity. An individual with cerebral palsy may have difficulty with fine motor tasks, such as writing or cutting with scissors; experience trouble with maintaining balance and walking; or be affected by involuntary movements, such as uncontrollable writhing motion of the hands or drooling. The symptoms differ from one person to the next, and may even change over time in the individual. Some people with cerebral palsy are also affected by other medical disorders, including seizures or mental impairment. Contrary to common belief, however, cerebral palsy does not always cause profound handicap. While a child with severe cerebral palsy might be unable to walk and need extensive, lifelong care, a child with mild cerebral palsy might only be slightly awkward and require no special assistance. Cerebral palsy is not contagious nor is it usually inherited from one generation to the next. At this time, it cannot be cured, although scientific research continues to yield improved treatments and methods of prevention.

How Many People Have This Disorder?

The United Cerebral Palsy Associations estimate that more than 500,000 Americans have cerebral palsy. Despite advances in preventing and treating certain causes of cerebral palsy, the number of children and adults it affects has remained essentially unchanged or perhaps risen slightly over the past 30 years. This is partly because more critically premature and frail infants are surviving through improved intensive care. Unfortunately, many of these infants have developmental problems of the nervous system or suffer neurological damage. Research is under way to improve care for these infants, as in ongoing studies of technology to alleviate troubled breathing and trials of drugs to prevent bleeding in the brain before or soon after birth.

What Are the Different Forms?

Spastic diplegia, the disorder first described by Dr. Little in the 1860s, is only one of several disorders called cerebral palsy. Today doctors classify cerebral palsy into four broad categories—spastic, athetoid, ataxic, and mixed forms—according to the type of movement disturbance.

Spastic cerebral palsy. In this form of cerebral palsy, which affects 70 to 80 percent of patients, the muscles are stiffly and permanently contracted. Doctors will often describe which type of spastic cerebral palsy a patient has based on which limbs are affected. The names given to these types combine a Latin description of affected limbs with the term plegia or paresis, meaning paralyzed or weak.

When both legs are affected by spasticity, they may turn in and cross at the knees. As these individuals walk, their legs move awkwardly and stiffly and nearly touch at the knees. This causes a characteristic walking rhythm, known as the scissors gait.Individuals with spastic hemiparesis may also experience hemiparetic tremors, in which uncontrollable shaking affects the limbs on one side of the body. If these tremors are severe, they can seriously impair movement.

Athetoid or dyskinetic cerebral palsy. This form of cerebral palsy is characterized by uncontrolled, slow, writhing movements. These abnormal movements usually affect the hands, feet, arms, or legs and, in some cases, the muscles of the face and tongue, causing grimacing or drooling. The movements often increase during periods of emotional stress and disappear during sleep. Patients may also have problems coordinating the muscle movements needed for speech, a condition known as dysarthria. Athetoid cerebral palsy affects about 10 to 20 percent of patients.

Ataxic cerebral palsy. This rare form affects the sense of balance and depth perception. Affected persons often have poor coordination; walk unsteadily with a wide-based gait, placing their feet unusually far apart; and experience difficulty when attempting quick or precise movements, such as writing or buttoning a shirt. They may also have intention tremor. In this form of tremor, beginning a voluntary movement, such as reaching for a book, causes a trembling that affects the body part being used and that worsens as the individual gets

nearer to the desired object. The ataxic form affects an esti-
mated 5 to 10 percent of cerebral palsy patients.

Mixed forms. It is common for patients to have symptoms
of more than one of the previous three forms. The most
common mixed form includes spasticity and athetoid movements but other combinations are also possible.

About the Author

JAMES GRIMM is forty years old and lives independently in New Hope, Minnesota. This is his first published book. Jim has given presentations to groups wanting to learn more about people with disabilities.